BOX
GIRL

BOX GIRL

My Part-Time Job as an Art Installation

LILIBET SNELLINGS

SOFT SKULL PRESS ▪ BERKELEY | AN IMPRINT OF COUNTERPOINT PRESS

Excerpt adapted from *Against The Machine: Being Human in the Age of the Electronic Mob* by Lee Siegel, copyright © 2008 by Lee Siegel. Used by permission of Spiegel & Grau, an imprint of The Random House Publishing Group, a division of Random House LLC. All rights reserved.

Hopscotch by Julio Cortazar, copyright © 1966. Used by permission of Random House LLC. All rights reserved

Library of Congress Cataloging-in-Publication Data

Snellings, Lilibet.
Box Girl : my part time job as an art installation / Lilibet Snellings.
pages cm
ISBN 978-1-59376-541-5 (pbk.)
1. Snellings, Lilibet. 2. Models (Persons)—California—Los Angeles—Biography. 3. Performance artists—California—Los Angeles--Biography. 4. Women performance artists—California—Los Angeles--Biography. 5. Los Angeles (Calif.)—Social life and customs. 6. Los Angeles (Calif.)—Biography. I. Title.
HD6073.M772U569 2014
702.81—dc23
[B]

2013028208

Cover Design: Jeff Miller, Faceout Studios
Interior Design: Neuwirth & Associates, Inc.

Soft Skull Press
An Imprint of Counterpoint
1919 Fifth Street
Berkeley, CA 94710
www.softskull.com

Printed in the United States of America
Distributed by Publishers Group West

10   9   8   7   6   5   4   3   2   1

FOR MY FAMILY.

And for Peter, my biggest cheerleader.
Literally. He is 6 foot 9.

California is a place in which a boom mentality and a sense of Chekhovian loss meet in uneasy suspension; in which the mind is troubled by some buried but ineradicable suspicion that things had better work here, because here, beneath that immense bleached sky, is where we run out of continent.

—JOAN DIDION,
"Notes from a Native Daughter"

[CONTENTS]

BOX
GIRL

Uniform

■

I take off my shoes first and crack my toes against the cold lobby floor. Then, I take off my jeans. Finally, my shirt. I am not naked, but close to it—in short white shorts and a tight white tank top. For the next seven hours, this is my uniform.

Reaching into my bag, I take out the things I want inside with me. Tonight it's my laptop, my phone, two pens, head-phones, this week's issue of *The New Yorker* even though I haven't opened last week's, a legal pad, lip gloss.

I comb my fingers through my hair, press my lips together, and glance quickly toward my feet, surveying my uniform, making sure everything important is covered. Finally, I re-trieve the stepladder, and, with my hands steadied on its sides, I climb up its stairs and crawl inside the box.

Box Girl Rule Sheet[1]

1. Every shift begins at 7:00 PM and ends at 2:00 AM. You must be inside the box at 7:00 PM promptly. Please arrive to the property by 6:45.[2]
2. You can take one thirty-minute break in the Employee Break Room and two bathroom breaks.
3. No food or drink inside the box.
4. Headphones are required if you are watching/listening to music.
5. No eye contact or relations with the guests or staff.
6. No socializing with guests or hotel employees before, during, or after your shift.
7. Don't touch the artwork in the box.

---

1 The actual rule sheet, provided by management.

2 At one point, the box shift was changed from 7:00 PM–2:00 AM to 6:00 PM–1:30 AM, and the pay was increased from $100 to $125/night. Then, during the recession, the shift was changed to 8:00 PM–12:00 AM, and the pay was cut to $60/night.

Uniforms:

1. The uniform is white boy shorts and white tank top. No alterations are acceptable.
2. Please wear undergarments.
3. Bring a robe, sweat pants, and flip-flops for breaks.
4. Makeup is light and natural.
5. Ultimately this is a modeling job and you must take care of your body. If you have severe bruises, bandages, or casts, you must wait until your body is healed and then ask to be put on the schedule.

Schedules:

1. If you are late twice in one month and you don't call the front desk to let them know, you will be taken off the schedule the following month. A no-show/no-call may result in a month's suspension or termination.
2. You must submit your availabilities by the twenty-fifth of each month for schedule placement consideration.
3. If someone calls you to cover her shift for her, you must not accept if you are already on the schedule for that week.
4. All shift changes must be relayed in writing via email to the Talent Coordinator. Text messages and phone calls are not acceptable.

General:

1. Valet your car. The front desk will take care of your parking for you.
2. Switch off the space heater before you leave at night.[3]

---

3 Another rule, which is absent from this list but I have seen on others, is "No sweatshirts, socks, or blankets." If a Box Girl gets cold, we are told, she can turn on a space heater, which is hidden below the mattress in a storage area. If she gets hot, she can turn on a fan, which is clipped to the ceiling and also hidden from the guests' view.

Please Wear Undergarments

■

I never thought I would be employed at a place where that needed to be put in writing.

The Box

Since The Standard Hotel opened on Sunset Boulevard in West Hollywood in 1998, a glass box with the dimensions of a large, waterless aquarium—fifteen feet long, four feet wide, five feet tall—has been a permanent art installation behind the front desk. Three sides of the box are glass, while the back wall, the one farthest from the lobby, is solid. The box is big enough for sitting, lying down, or sleeping, but about a foot too short for standing.

Inside the box, there is only a single mattress with white, starch-smelling sheets tucked and folded crisply at its corners. On top of that, there is one firm pillow. Two, if I'm lucky.

In front of the box is the concierge desk: a minimalist block of glossy off-white. In front of that are three backless barstools, which no one ever sits on. The floor in the lobby is an eggshell shade too, shiny like it's just been shellacked with a coat of clear nail polish. Five succulent plants—four that look like legitimate cacti, one that looks more like a desert tree—line the left side of the lobby, a wall of white tiles behind them. Below the plants' polished white pots, five piles of broken sea glass undulate like a shattered wave. To the right, slouchy brown chairs are clustered in various combinations—two facing each other, six side-by-side to create the effect of a couch. Beneath them, there's a white shag rug, which is no longer white, and no longer shaggy, but a matted-down gray. A waterfall of pale beads cascades from the ceiling in one corner, and four large silver lamps dip their necks like giraffes toward the center of the room. Their globular metallic heads look like dryers at the hair salon, or something out of *The Jetson's* living room.

This lobby is not sure if it's from the future or the past. It's mod in the modernist space-age sense, like what we thought the future was going to look like in the 1950s. In the corner, a maid is dressed like Alice from *The Brady Bunch*, wearing a pressed, pink uniform with a Peter Pan collar. She sprays Windex on an acrylic bubble chair, which dangles from a chain.

Automatic sliding-glass doors open onto the hotel's valet area, where a sign that reads *The Standard* hangs purposefully upside down. Giant *Jurassic Park* leaves obscure an unattractive stretch of Sunset Boulevard across the street: a 1970s-style beige office building; a parking lot (ten dollars during the day, twenty at night); a Guess billboard featuring a model gyrating in the sand, wearing a pair of jeans and a denim jacket; and a Cabo Cantina, which looks like it's decorated for Cinco de Mayo every day of the year.

During the day, the scene in the lobby rarely changes. Everyone always seems to be waiting for someone else. A man fidgets with his phone. A woman jangles the bracelets on her wrist, digging for a watch under an armful of accessories.

But by dusk, as the smell of chlorine surrenders to cigarette smoke, the set begins to change. Every night, at seven o'clock, the Box Girl arrives. From 7:00 PM to 2:00 AM, she can do whatever she wants inside the box—read, talk on her phone, use her computer, even sleep. The only thing she absolutely cannot do is make eye contact with anyone outside the box. It is supposed to appear as if this mysterious creature has no idea anyone else is around. No clue that anyone is out there, looking in.

Once a week, I am that mysterious creature.

Could You Tidy It Up a Bit?

■

I would like to think I'm a fairly responsible Box Girl: I arrive on time; I wear undergarments; I have never shown up to a shift with my leg in a cast. Yet tonight, I find myself reprimanded, the recipient of my very first Box Girl demerit.

It's a few hours into the night when the concierge swings open the door, which he never does, so I am sufficiently startled. He takes in the view: me, the mattress, my stuff.

"You're not supposed to have so much stuff in the box at once," he says. "Only one thing at a time."

I guess this is an unwritten rule.

I am, in fact, surrounded. To my left, my laptop. To my right, my phone. Next to that, three books, two spiral-bound notepads, a blue pen, two black pens, headphones, hand cream, a nail file, and my electricity bill. On the periphery, countless pieces of paper are wadded into frustrated little fists. It looks like my apartment. It looks real. It looks *too* real.

"Could you tidy it up a bit?" he says. "It looks messy."

Well this is mildly mortifying.

"Oh my god, of course," I say, groping for the most overtly disposable items. A colony of notebook-paper balls has assembled like dust bunnies where the mattress meets the glass. I crunch the pieces of paper together, unsuccessfully attempting to create one humongous sphere, and start stacking my stuff.

Did he say I was only allowed to have one thing in here? Only one? Which thing will it be? Obviously it will be the computer, but what if I want the book? While I know I can only do one thing at a time, I'd like to at least have the option of some other distraction.

My Natural Habitat

∎

It's been documented that animals in captivity exhibit some very bizarre behaviors. Primates, for example, often eat and throw their own feces. They are also known to engage in a behavior called "regurgitation and reingestion"—vomiting into their hands and then eating the vomit. While I have never thrown my own feces or voluntarily reingested my own vomit, I can say, with certainty, that how one acts while stuck inside a cage is most definitely not how one acts when left to one's own free will.

We are told to behave in the box as if we are alone in our living rooms. First of all, I don't have a living room. And if I did, when I sat in it, I wouldn't make sure I was sitting in a way that doesn't make my thighs look fat. I wouldn't continually untangle my hair with my fingers. I wouldn't make sure my lip gloss was not smudged outside my lip area. I do not wear lip gloss at home.

Observed in my one-room apartment, I'd most likely be wearing my other uniform: a greenish-yellow sweatshirt that most closely resembles the color of diarrhea, pajama pants that are too short, and tube socks that are too tall. If it was chilly, I might have a powder blue bathrobe over that. My hair would be piled into a hay-like heap on top of my head, and I probably would not have shaved my legs even to my knee—forget the elevations my razor has to ascend before a box shift.

I'd be sitting on my bed, surrounded by a smattering of books and magazines—a *New Yorker* from weeks before (they just come *so* frequently), an *In Touch* from that week—and a variety of items not meant to be on bed sheets: a laptop, a jar of nail polish, various crumbly snacks. I'd probably be neglecting it all while turning up the volume on the latest episode of *Extreme Couponing*.

Not only does my apartment not have a living room, it also does not have a bedroom. Technically, a studio does not have a bedroom, a living room, or a kitchen. It's just one large room having an identity crisis. I can basically open my front door while in the shower. To make matters worse, my address has a half in it—316 ½—the studio apartment's bastard stepchild. The ½ handle is very confusing for delivery people, and thus very inconvenient for me, a delivery enthusiast.

"No," I say, to the Domino's order-taker, "I'm not the house in the front; I'm up the stairs in the back." More often than not, my downstairs neighbor has to bring my pizza up to me, which was particularly embarrassing the time I had already fallen asleep and didn't remember I had ordered pizza in the first place.

Startled awake by the knocking, I tripped toward the door, disoriented and lacking pants.

"Who is it?" I said through the door.

"Your pizza's here," the voice answered.

"My what?" I said, pinching the corners of my eyes, trying to extract some moisture from my contacts.

"Your pizza!" the voice was shouting now.

"Who is this?" I said, wishing this person would go away.

"It's Ken! From downstairs!"

"Oh, hey Ken," I said, relieved, and still through the door. "No listen I'm good, I don't want any pizza, but thanks though."

"No, I'm not offering you pizza," he said. "You ordered pizza and it was delivered to our house."

"Oh right, yeah, *obviously*. I was totally just messing with you. Want a slice?"

Or perhaps an observer might catch me during the day, sitting at my desk, my left foot propped up on my chair, my chin perched on top of my knee. I'd probably be peeling the polish off my nails while staring at the blinking cursor of a blank Microsoft Office document, *blink, blink, blink*. Like staring into the refrigerator, hoping something will magically appear for me.

Maybe, on that particular day, I had decided that wearing a hat might make me more focused. But which hat? They were all so disorganized. *Maybe I should organize them*, I might have thought. It's amazing all the things I suddenly realize I need to do when I am supposed to be doing something else. *Maybe*, I might have thought, *since I'm up, I should water that plant? Maybe I should tweeze my eyebrows? Maybe I should go through my closet and see what old jeans might make good cut-offs? Maybe I should make a pair of cut-offs and wear them while I Clorox the bathroom? Maybe I'll bleach the shower in my new shorts, which will be both stylish and utilitarian, and then I'll have to open every window because of the fumes, have to determine the apartment a biohazard, and be forced to evacuate immediately and seek shelter at the bar down the street, where the air is much safer and where there happens to be a very reasonable Happy Hour going on.*

One might observe *that* process, were they to see me alone in my lack of living room. But no lip gloss.

Hello, Box Talent!

At the end of each month, all the Box Girls receive an emailed schedule marked with the red exclamation point that indicates "High Priority." These emails typically open with the salutation, "Hello, Box Talent!" A curious phrase for a job that requires no talent. This mass message reminds us that a Box Girl can only work once a week. This is to keep variety. If a guest is staying at the hotel for, say, five days, he'll see a different girl each day—The Blonde Box Girl, The Brunette Box Girl, The Asian Box Girl, The Hispanic Box Girl, The Black Box Girl, and so on—like his very own bag of Box Girl Skittles.

For a short while, I think there was a Box Boy, though I heard he was very androgynous. Then again, I have no idea what he looked like, or what any of the other Box People do either. Our schedules never overlap; I get their texts and emails asking to cover shifts, but aside from that, they are as faceless to me as the maids who turn down the sheets. The Standard hosted a Christmas party one year, but it was still hard to tell. Is she a Box Girl? Is she? Is she a random guest? A hotel employee? Everyone in West Hollywood looks so similar anyway. It was impossible to know.

Prep

■

My 1989 BMW sputters into The Standard's valet driveway and takes its place in line with BMWs from this century. An eager young man in a snug-fitting shirt asks if I'm a guest of the hotel.

"Box Girl," I say, while gathering my things from the passenger-side seat.

"Oh, right!" he says, pretending to recognize me. I am sure we all start to look the same after a while.

The valets are all very fit young men. Actors, presumably. *Aspiring* actors. The service industry in Los Angeles has got to be one of the best looking, whitest-toothed bunches in the world. (Sometimes, during breaks from the box, I'll strike up a conversation with another employee in the cafeteria—a valet, a bellhop, a room service deliverer. "So what brought you to LA?" I'll ask, while sucking down a Diet Coke and shoving a handful of dry cereal in my mouth. Every time the answer is the same: acting.)

The guy in the snug-fitting shirt gets in my car and hands me a valet ticket.

I head to the bathroom, which is my first stop, always. I brush my hair, put on lip gloss, and apply thigh-firming lotion. Then I smile and pick whatever food I ate on the way to the hotel out of my teeth. Tonight it's a peanut-butter-and-honey sandwich, and I'm kicking myself for forgetting a toothbrush, again, since a large portion of the sandwich still seems to be stuck in the sides of my mouth.

A deejay is setting up her equipment in a booth to the left of the box. This is a relief. For about a year, there was live music in the lobby bar. Music is a stretch. I am no songbird, but this singer must have been friends with someone who worked at the hotel because there is no way anyone would have booked this person based on his abilities. He sounded like a dying whale, or maybe a whale sending a mating call. I'm not sure if there's a huge difference. Every Wednesday, without fail, he'd do this rendition of Radiohead's "High and Dry" that could peel the paint off the walls.

When I leave for the night, the valet will tell me my tires are dangerously bald.

"Thanks," I'll say. "I'll get those checked."

"No, not checked," he'll say. "You need *new tires*."

An Emotional Detroit

■

My dad still sends clippings the old-fashioned way. Not by forwarding a link, but by digging scissors out of his desk, cutting out an article, circling the important parts, stuffing it in a manila envelope, and driving to the post office. It's one of his many endearing Andy Rooney-esque quirks.

While cleaning out my desk, I came across a photocopied page from a 2006 issue of *Forbes*. It was a list of famous quotes about Los Angeles, and at the top of the page, in my dad's all-caps scrawl, it said: *FOR L.A. PIG, LOVE DAD.* (He's always called me "Pig" or "Porkchop" or some other member of the swine family.) At the time that he mailed this, I had been living in LA for almost two years. He put a star next to his favorites:

* "*California is a fine place to live—if you happen to be an orange.*"

    —FRED ALLEN

* "*Hollywood: An emotional Detroit.*"

    —LILLIAN GISH

* *"Only remember—west of the Mississippi it's a little more look, see, act. A little less rationalize, comment, talk."*

—F. SCOTT FITZGERALD

* *"Living in Hollywood is like living in a lit cigarette butt."*

—PHYLLIS DILLER

* *"Fall is my favorite season in Los Angeles, watching the birds change color and fall from the trees."*

—DAVID LETTERMAN

As I re-read these quotes I could hear my dad laughing—just howling, his high-pitched honk of a laugh—as he scratched each asterisk into the page.

Oh the Horror

■

Los Angeles is not a place I ever thought I would reside. Growing up on the East Coast, in very comfortable corners of Georgia and Connecticut, LA—or La La Land, or Hollywood—was not a place you lived. If anything, it was a place you read about in the tabloids and made fun of. In the beginning, when people asked why I moved here, I said I lost a bet. In actuality the decision was much less impulsive than that: It was decided over a couple bottles of white wine while eating lunch.

To my dad's horror and utter bewilderment, he and my mom (a chemical engineering major with an MBA and the recipient of a master's degree in biology, respectively) raised two English majors. My dad was successful in the pulp and paper business and retired very young. My mom is hard-working in her own right, with the framed certificate in our laundry room to prove it: "Connecticut Volunteer of The Year." My parents were not ones to put a lot of pressure on their children—it wasn't like we *had* to grow up to do this, or *had* to become a "that," but there were still certain unspoken expectations. My brother at least took his BA in English down a lucrative tract: He worked on Wall Street, got an MBA, and ended up back in New York, where he works in finance. While my parents knew I loved to write, they assumed I would also move to New York and get a job in publishing. I had assumed the same thing. Thus I spent all summer after graduation living at home in Connecticut, attending informational interviews in Manhattan, not knowing that "informational" means, "We don't have a job for you, but we'll give you ten minutes of our time." I spent these meetings fielding comments like, "University of Colorado, huh? Big party school I hear," while shifting uneasily in ill-fitting pantsuits from Ann Taylor Loft.

Late that summer, I went to Los Angeles with Heather, my best friend from college, to visit our other best friend, Rachel. Heather and Rachel were also living with their parents, looking for jobs: Heather in the suburbs of Chicago, Rachel in a suburb of LA. Frustrated by the incessant refreshing of our Hotmail inboxes and the waiting helplessly to hear from jobs we'd applied to on Monster.com, Heather and I had decided a weeklong vacation in LA was just what the therapist ordered.

Everything about Los Angeles was intoxicating on that inaugural trip. The whole place seemed dream-like, foreign, and fabulous, if not a little bit filthy. I was certain I was going to see a celebrity as soon as I got off the plane. Rachel was our tour guide, and she took us to the Santa Monica Pier, the Venice Boardwalk, the Sky Bar on Sunset Boulevard. As the week went on, an idea began brewing: Why did Heather and I have to get a job in our hometowns' neighboring metropolises? Why would we split up when we could cling to each other while entering adulthood? "Let's just move here!" We threw it out there, but we knew we never would. We were too scared—to tell our parents, to leave the boyfriends and lives and expectations that were waiting for us back home.

Yet, on the penultimate day of our trip, during a late lunch at The Farm in Beverly Hills, something shifted. Maybe it was the sunshine, maybe it was the Sauvignon Blanc, but giddy and high on friendship and wine, the decision was made: "Let's move here. Let's really move here." The three of us could get a place together. We decided we had to call our parents immediately, before we changed our minds. I walked to the corner of Beverly and Santa Monica Boulevards—an intersection I cannot pass without remembering this excruciating conversation—and told my parents I was moving three time zones and 2,963 miles west; as far from Connecticut as I possibly could without wading into the Pacific.

Within three weeks, Heather and I had moved across the country, with no jobs, no cars, and no place to live. This nearly broke my sweet, Southern mother's heart. (Both my parents are originally from Georgia, with the accents to prove it.) She had assumed I would get a job in Manhattan, of course. California might as well have been another country in my parents' minds. And Los Angeles, oh the horror. At least San Francisco was *tolerable*, they'd say. Soon after I moved, my mom called to tell me she had to close the door to my bedroom. "I just couldn't bear to look at it, knowing you are so far away."

The first few weeks we lived in LA, we didn't really live in LA at all, but rather with Rachel's parents in a San Fernando Valley suburb called Encino. We were familiar with Brendan Fraser in *Encino Man,* but not this city where Michael Jackson grew up. We quickly learned that it was not such a bad spot to be stuck in late summer while looking for a job. Rachel's parents' house was a sprawling, contemporary take on the Southern California ranch house. It had a large, slate-tile hot tub, an eco-friendly saltwater pool, and a variety of California vegetables growing in the yard, not to mention all the home-cooked food and expensive wine we could consume.

Most of our job-search period was spent in the pool. Once or twice a day, I'd flutter-kick to the shallow end, peel my waterlogged limbs off my inflatable raft, twist a towel under my arms, and shuffle inside to refresh my email on their boxy, beige desktop, my hair dripping onto the keyboard. (This was 2004, when checking your email enlisted more physical labor than just rolling over on a chaise lounge and shading your iPhone's screen from the sun.) Realizing I'd gotten no responses to my job inquiries, I'd grab an organic Popsicle from the freezer and hurry back poolside to avoid getting chilled from the air conditioning.

Unfortunately, after three weeks, we found jobs. We moved to Santa Monica because it was the only part of LA any of us had ever heard of, and I'm fairly certain that had something to do with a late-'90s Sheryl Crow song. Our apartment building was a shutter-less stucco box, painted a shade of warm salmon, the address written in loopy, spearmint cursive. It looked like something out of Sinatra-era Palm Springs, just shittier. We were pleasantly surprised to find the windows had no screens, because apparently there are no bugs in California, but less pleased to learn the apartment came with no refrigerator, because apparently LA renters are expected to lug those along as if they were fresh towels or a new set of sheets.

There is a whole underground market for used refrigerators in LA. We found ours on Craigslist, where we found most everything those days—our couch, a coffee table, my 1989 BMW convertible with a CD player that skipped when I drove over bumps. Armed with a wad of cash, which was no doubt split three ways—as if we planned on dividing the fridge three ways when we moved into our own one-bedroom apartments a year later—we met the sellers on a manicured corner of San Vicente Boulevard. (For at least a year, we called San Vicente and Abbott Kinney "The Bermuda Triangle" because, unlike every other street in LA that shoots pin-straight until eternity, these boulevards defiantly existed on diagonals, crissing and crossing other sane streets, leaving virgin LA drivers like us feeling as though we'd just been spun around blindfolded before a whack at the piñata.)

The refrigerator transaction took place on a Sunday morning. As the couple waited for us, a handsome dog panted alongside, attached to a leash that had been needle-pointed with someone's initials. They looked like they had just finished a workout. Probably a hike. Twenty minutes late, we rolled up in various shades of hungover. I think it's a decent bet that at least one of us wasn't wearing a bra. The couple stood there smiling with their fridge, which was on a dolly. They owned a dolly. They said their new place came with its own fridge. Of course it did. They were in their late twenties, maybe early thirties—it was hard to tell back then—and they clearly had their shit together. I wiped under my eyes to remove the remnants of last night's mascara and wondered if I'd ever be that put together on a Sunday morning. I bet they had already read *The New York Times*. Probably over a soy latte at an impossibly hip, fair-trade coffee shop after their hike.

But we weren't quite sure how to be adults yet. Our four years at The University of Colorado (we affectionately called it The Harvard of The Rockies) hadn't armed us with much but liberal arts degrees and a superhuman ability to funnel beers at a high altitude. I studied journalism, which I'm not even sure is a major anymore; Rachel majored in painting, and I'll leave that at that; and Heather majored in the "smart" slacker specialty: sociology. A few weeks before our pre-move trip to LA, Heather had a meeting with a career counselor and took one of those aptitude tests that says what you should do with the rest of your life. She called me crying from the parking lot immediately after. Through the crying/hyperventilating/mini panic attack that is the wheelhouse of recent grads, she said the counselor told her that she didn't really have any career options, and that she probably should have thought about that before she decided to major in sociology. And that she should just go kill herself. (Heather added that part.)

■

Shortly after we moved into our apartment, a Penske truck arrived with all of our belongings: whatever furniture was salvageable after four years of "Jungle Juice" parties in Boulder, our favorite books, framed pictures of our families, and five-pound Case Logics of CDs housing our entire music collections, which were nothing if not varied. (You know you're a child of the '90s when you can say you listened to the Grateful Dead and Bone Thugs-N-Harmony with equal gusto.) While unpacking boxes of "necessities"—the enormous black stereo with the equally sizable speakers attached by a tangle of wires, the Halloween costumes that only follow you across a continent when you're twenty-two and think that makes sense—we began to assemble our new adult lives. Or some pathetic attempt at them.

This was around the time I convinced my friend Melissa to move to LA, too. Melissa and I grew up in Connecticut together, and she spent her first four un-chaperoned years attending Georgetown University, getting a good education. Thus, she already had a job in New York. I had promised her that as soon as I found a job, we'd get an apartment together in the city. Well, I told her on the phone from California, I never found a job there, so instead I moved to LA, a mere three time zones away. This wouldn't be a big deal, right? We could still live together! We have a great house! There's plenty of room for you! Your job will transfer you, right? Great. Pick you up at the Long Beach Jet Blue terminal in what, a week? Super.

Shockingly, after a week of not returning my calls because she was so livid, Melissa caved and said yes. It was now September and she had been living at home since May, making the hour commute from Connecticut to midtown Manhattan via Metro North. Earlier that summer, we met during her lunch break, and I inquired where she had purchased that snazzy navy skirt suit. She told me Talbots, and then said, "My life is over." During that phone call from California, I might have mentioned that no one wears skirt suits out here. I didn't even think they had Talbots. I also think I mentioned the words "beach" and "cute boys." With that, she was packing up her Case Logic, too.

To create space for Melissa, Heather and I decided to share a room. The master was enormous, and our rent would be cheaper that way. As if two twenty-two-year-old women sharing a bedroom wasn't juvenile enough, one of the first things we both unboxed were our teddy bears, which we immediately perched atop our peach and purple pillows. Heather's bear was named Amie, after the Pure Prairie League song "Amie." (Heather and her mom were obsessed with the softer side of late-'70s rock. Heather once punched me in the arm, pretty damn hard, when I casually mentioned that Jackson Browne sucked.) My furry friend, Gundy, was not named after a song but after his brand, Gund. Not my most creative moment. It's not that surprising; I was never particularly kind to my inanimate friends as a child. All my Barbies got brutal haircuts within the first few weeks I plied them from their plastic wombs, and one night, my brother and I lynched my largest baby doll with a noose made of shoelaces. We hung her out my bedroom window, swinging triumphantly in front of the dining room window, while our parents were mid–dinner party.

As a child, I also had to sleep with absolutely no light—not even the slightest crack creeping under the door—while *The Nutcracker* soundtrack played on my robot-shaped cassette player. Looking back, I realize this was sort of unsettling music for a child before bedtime. In the room with Heather, it wasn't *The Nutcracker* that unnerved me, but "Cinnamon Girl" by Neil Young, the first few bars of which played full-blast every morning at 6:45 from her CD-player alarm clock. I still can't hear the song's beginning chords without feeling an overwhelming impulse to get in the shower.

It was hard to believe we ever complained about 11:00 am classes. As it turned out, with real jobs, you had to show up much earlier than that. Every day. And not still wearing the shirt you slept in with a Patagonia fleece zipped over it. Melissa's company transferred her position in marketing to their office on Wilshire Boulevard. I took a job as an assistant at a talent agency, and Rachel got a job as a personal assistant, working for a woman who ended up being certifiably insane. By winter, Rachel had become suspicious that this woman might just be using her for a free place to stay in Park City during Sundance. Rachel finally quit in the spring when one of the woman's checks bounced and, in what we can plainly call the final straw, the woman's toddler son peed on her during a business trip to Berkeley. Heather got a toddler-free job as the receptionist at a post-production office, where she is now a producer and makes more money than all of us. (Take that, career counselor.)

At the post-production office, one of Heather's responsibilities was ordering lunch and dinner for the clients, who were stuck in bays editing commercials all day. She ordered from the best restaurants in Santa Monica, and she always ordered way too much. She *must* have done this intentionally—*well played, Heather*—because almost every night, she'd arrive home with giant catering containers and zip-locked bags full of gourmet leftovers. Sometimes, if it were someone's birthday, the vast majority of a very large sheet cake would make it into our kitchen. The four of us would sit on the couch, free food on our laps, watching *So You Think You Can Dance* while drinking mugs full of Yellowtail Shiraz purchased from the CVS down the street. (Why was it always mugs at that age? Why didn't we ever have clean and/or proper glassware?) We went out to bars some nights, went out to dinner even less. We were paralyzed by the fear of managing our own money for the first time, and even more terrified of being hungover at work.

The mornings were miserable enough. Rachel and I sometimes carpooled to work, and she started calling my evil morning alter ego "Lilly," after the name I'd give the Starbucks baristas to write on my cup. I've never understood why Starbucks employees don't realize their early-morning customers have not yet had their early-morning coffee and are not yet perky or peppy enough to chat. If I ran a Starbucks, I would tell my employees that, before 9:00 am, they had to be grumpy and irritable. It's much more relatable.

Most days, "Lilly" drove to work by herself. My roommates would cheerfully announce that they had gotten all of their East Coast phone calls done on the way to work. But in the morning, I didn't want to talk to anyone. Some mornings I'd listen to music on the radio, or to NPR, or, more mornings than not, nothing. Just staring, in silence, at the endless bumpers before me. The agency's office was off of Wilshire Boulevard in Beverly Hills. Those first few weeks during the drive from Santa Monica to Beverly Hills, every sign I passed seemed like a prop in a film. Beverly Hills wasn't a real place, was it? And Rodeo Drive? I mean, come on, that was just where Julia Roberts went shopping in *Pretty Woman*. Even Wilshire Boulevard sounded sort of regal, not at all real. It was disorienting and, though I desperately tried to suppress it, depressing.

During those first months in LA I reported back fanatically to friends and family on the East Coast:

"I absolutely love it!" I'd say.

"We live only blocks from the beach!" (Twenty-six.)

"I can ride my bike everywhere!" (I didn't even have a bike.)

"Traffic? Ha! I haven't seen a bit!"

I concocted these lies because I couldn't bear to admit the truth: many a morning, I welled up thinking about the leaves on the trees in Connecticut. It was October, and I desperately missed fall foliage. I missed leaves of any color, for that matter. I missed *trees*. I thought for the first several months that the thermometer in my car was broken because it always said 73. I hated the sameness. I hated that it was always sunny. I wanted it to rain. Though I had abandoned my longing for a cozy wool sweater, I wanted to at least be able to wear pants. Or put on a pair of socks. While my East Coast friends were wrapped in fleece watching football, I was sticking to my seat in stop-and-go traffic. I thought nothing was more depressing than mid-day, mid-week in Los Angeles—so hot, so bright, too still—nothing but sharp angles and exaggerated shadows. High noon was an unsettling, sunshine-y nightmare, and I totally, completely hated it.

Bam

■

Like a zookeeper, the concierge comes to shut me in the box. There's no handle on the inside, so I can't shut myself in. The door always seems swollen, no matter what the weather, and requires a rather startling *BAM* to shut.

After placing my book, laptop, and notepad in a neat stack (if I am going to break the "one item at a time" rule, I figure I need to keep it tidy), I tap on the glass to get the concierge's attention. He turns around, and I write with an imaginary pen in the air. He nods, then writes the hotel's Wi-Fi code on a piece of paper and holds it up to the glass. I jot it down on my yellow legal pad and give him a thumbs-up.

I enter the Wi-Fi code. It doesn't work. I enter it again. Still, nothing. I knock quietly on the glass. No one notices. I knock louder. No one notices. I knock again, this time really rapping on the thing. People in the lobby probably think the Box Girl is having some sort of emergency. And you know what? I *am* having some sort of emergency. There is no way I am sitting in here for seven hours with no Wi-Fi. The concierge turns around. I wave toward myself and mouth, "Come here for a second." He jerks open the door and I tell him the code won't work. He goes back to the front desk and returns a minute later, explaining that he forgot a number when he wrote it down the first time.

I didn't mean to cause a scene, but I cannot sit in here for seven hours with no Internet. I will go crazy.

But maybe without it, I'd actually finish a book. Maybe, come to think of it, it would be like a seven-hour vacation. Maybe I'll take this piece of paper with the Wi-Fi code and use it as a bookmark. That's what I'll do. Watch me go. I'll be done with this book in no time.

■

I read a page and a half. I am distracted because my laptop is staring at me. That little slit on its side is "breathing" its creepy electronic breath at me. Also, the Apple logo looks so strange from this angle. Had I ever noticed there was a bite taken out of it? I don't think I had. My laptop looks so funny all folded up like that; I rarely see it closed. It's so slender when it's shut. Like a rectangular silver clam. A clam with wonderful little pearls of procrastination inside. A clam with . . . okay, enough with this clam metaphor. Just give me the damn laptop.

I reach for it. I open it. It lights itself up, so delighted to see me. I shut it. I'm not doing it.

I read three pages. The stupid computer is still breathing at me. Its breath seems labored. Is it dying? Is it lonely over there?

I bookmark my page with the piece of paper with the Wi-Fi code on it. I open the laptop. I retrieve the piece of paper from book and enter the Wi-Fi code. I click on Safari and I start to scroll. The lines have been cut. I am officially untethered. I'm out to sea.

Now the book looks abandoned, shoved behind the mattress. I pick it up, caress its cover as if to say, "I'm sorry," and use it to prop up my laptop.

The Various Positions in My Rotation

Typically, when I first get inside the box, I slide onto my stomach and face my laptop with my legs crossed at the ankles. Reaching behind me, I pull out my hair so it spills over my shoulders. I wipe the excess lip gloss from the corners of my mouth and rub what I removed into the back of my hand because there is nowhere else to wipe it. I get my shorts just so. I like the elastic band rolled over and hiked down so a sliver of skin shows between the bottom of my shirt and the top of my shorts. I've decided this is slimming. I'll stay this way for about a half hour—until my back or elbows or neck or all three begin to ache.

There's no perfect position in the box. Without a chair, I'm working with a very limited set of options, and the most comfortable positions are not the most flattering. The ergonomically-correct-yet-aesthetically-pleasing tango is sort of a nightmare.

Thus, I have outlined some of my favorite yoga-inspired box positions. Except I don't do yoga, so I have a very limited knowledge of the poses. I think there's one about a dog and one about a child, but other than that, they all look like some sort of one-legged bird to me. But don't despair, I can work around this, and with practice and patience, even you can master the most challenging Box Girl poses.

The Slender Typist

We'll assign this name to the dependable default position I described above. For the yogis out there, this position is reminiscent of "chaturanga" (I looked that up), except you will find it much easier than chaturanga because you in no way have to hold yourself up. This position engages absolutely no muscles and is definitely bad for your neck.

> *PROS:* Slimming.
> *CONS:* Neck pain, elbow numbness, loss of feeling in fingertips.

The Indian Princess

For this pose, sit facing the front of the box with your legs crossed in the position formerly known as "Indian style." (I hear nursery school teachers are now going with the more politically correct "pretzel style.") This pose is akin to the "lotus" position in yoga (I think), except you don't have to fold your feet up on top of your thighs because that would be weird. Thus, you will find it much more comfortable. Once in the position-formerly-known-as-Indian-style, place your laptop on your lap. While this pose risks exposing a certain private area, it can be sustained for many hours.

PROS: Good for typing over prolonged periods of time.
CONS: Crotch shot. Laptop can get very hot on bare legs.
Makes you look sort of squatty. See also: neck pain.

The Downward Reader, with the Side-Reader Variation

The Downward Reader is an excellent option if you are reading something that is lightweight, like a paperback or a Kindle. This position is very simple: Lie on your back and hold your book in front of your face. This pose cannot be sustained for very long, however, because your arms will get very tired. First, they will feel hot, then heavy, and then eventually like lead. Plus you will sort of look like a dipshit holding a book right in front of your face. If you are experiencing any of these sensations, I'd suggest moving into the Side-Reader Variation pose. For this, roll onto your side, lean your weight on one forearm, and hold your book in the corresponding hand. This will free up your other hand to turn the pages. This position comes in handy if you are reading something heavy. Unfortunately, after about fifteen minutes, the supporting arm will start to tingle, and after an hour, it will go completely numb.

PROS: Slimming. Reading is good for you.
CONS: Loss of circulation to arms. Possibility of looking like a dipshit.

The Sleeping Booty

The box-adapted sleep poses will remind you most of the end of a yoga class. Sleeping positions in the box are tricky.

There are four variations, none of them good. You can lie on your back, but I wouldn't recommend it. You will look like you're dead. (Consequently, this is called the "corpse" position in yoga.) This will be alarming for guests. You can lie on your stomach, but this is not very comfortable, and hasn't your mother ever told you it gives you wrinkles? You can lie on your side, and face the lobby in a borderline fetal position, but then your open mouth is also facing the lobby, which is awkward if you drool and/or snore. Unless you look like the people in the Lunesta commercials when you sleep, I wouldn't recommend this position. You can lie on your side and face the back wall in said fetal position, though while your drooling and snoring mouth will be hidden, your butt will be on display for the entire lobby.

PROS: Sleep is good for you.
CONS: Too many to list. Drink an espresso before your shift.

The Nutcracker

The Nutcracker is an emergency position that was developed in a moment of desperation. When it was "that time of the month," I got my shift covered for reasons so obvious, they need not be stated here. One incredibly unfortunate night, however, I got my period *while* I was in the box and had to ask the male concierge if he could find me a tampon. For the rest of the night, I sat with my legs sealed together like a wooden nutcracker doll. This pose is very confusing for hotel guests who will wonder why you haven't moved from the same position for several hours. Some might even wonder if you are, in fact, made of wood.

PROS: Good for posture. Strengthens lower back.
CONS: Mortifying. Confusing to hotel guests. See also:
mortifying.

The No-Show, aka The Called-in-Fat

Say it's Super Bowl Monday, say it's the Wednesday after Christmas, say it's a regular Tuesday. It doesn't matter. This get-out-of-jail-free-card can be cashed in whenever you need it. If your thighs are not feeling quite toned enough for the unforgiving overhead lights, fear not. We've all been there. Pretend you have an audition. A very late audition that doesn't start until eight o'clock. This is the yoga equivalent of not showing up to class.

PROS: You can sit in whatever position you want in
your real living room.
CONS: You feel fat.

The Sly Pick

In the event you have any sort of itch to itch or wedgie to pick, you must do this very discreetly. I suggest fixing these things on the fly, while transitioning from one position to the next.

PROS: Problem solved. Comfort.
CONS: There's really no subtle way to pick your wedgie in
a glass box under a spotlight. I am just trying to make
you feel better.

She's Got a Good Booty for a White Girl

■

People in the lobby assume I can't hear them when I'm in the box. Perhaps it's from watching too many crime-scene TV shows, but there is something about a glassed-in room that makes people assume it's soundproof.

It's not.

If I choose to listen, I can hear everything. I can hear the drunk couple at the end of the night—her hanging on his arm like a koala on a branch—asking how much for a room for the night. I can hear the group of guys debating between The Sky Bar, the Chateau Marmot, or the strip club, as well as the unanimous decision: "Strip club. Done."

Most interestingly, I can hear any and all commentary about "that girl in the box." Me.

Tourists, especially those with Southern accents, seem to ask the most questions. They'll lean forward on the front desk, their bags still slung over their shoulders, and demand to know, "Well how in the hell long is she in there for?"

Sometimes, concerned parents ask, "Is it hard to breathe in there?"

But, the most-asked question by far is, "Can they go to the bathroom?"

When anyone finds out I'm a Box Girl, this is always the first thing they want to know. It is such a ludicrous question, I can't resist giving a ludicrous answer: "No."

"Are you serious?" they'll ask. "For how *long*?"

"Seven hours," I'll say.

"What?" they'll demand. "How do you do that?"

"Some Box Girls go in their pants, but I prefer to avoid liquid for twenty-four hours prior to my shift. Just dry out like a raisin," I'll say.

Of course we are allowed to go to the bathroom.

Like the questions, I also hear a lot of observations about, well, myself. One night, a young African American guy leaned over the counter and said to the male concierge, "She's got a good booty for a white girl." I lay there on my stomach, my booty behind me, stadium-like lights shining down upon it, and stared at my book, frozen. I didn't know whether to laugh or cry. Though I'm no expert, I'm fairly certain this means I have a "large" booty for a white girl.

I much prefer the question I'll hear if I'm lying very, very still: "Is she real?"

This always makes me happy because I know mannequins don't have cellulite.

Underdog

■

My legs looked like a Jackson Pollock painting: several sharp slashes of red here (cuts from various thorny things), a drizzle of dots there (mosquito bites), a mysterious patch of puffy pinkness (poison ivy, probably). I emailed the box coordinator to get my shift covered. I didn't explain why, saying only, "I don't feel well." I felt fine. But the problem was too hard to explain, especially to someone in Los Angeles, where there is no grass. My legs were torn up because my dad had asked me to mow the lawn a few days before, while I was home in Connecticut.

My dad, firmly planted in the one percent, cuts his own grass. He says it's good exercise, but let's be honest: It's because he doesn't want to pay anyone else to do it. He is an old-school man who's worked for every dollar he's ever had and refuses to waste a penny of it. My dad mows his own grass, drives his cars until the doors fall off, and organizes his own garbage to take to the dump.

While he is happy to spend money on things he really cares about—family, food, golf, a good Scotch—he absolutely loathes wasted money. Hell hath no fury like my father when he found out a Blockbuster movie was turned in late and we were charged an extra dollar per day.

He asked me to cut the grass because he had recently undergone knee surgery and couldn't do it himself. His knee had been injured during a misunderstanding with a purebred Newfoundland in The Hamptons. He and my mom were spending a weekend with some friends who have a summerhouse in Southampton, and my dad was doing some late afternoon laps in the pool. Apparently his style of swimming—the two-armed flailing with a modified frog kick, which he calls "the backstroke"—alarmed the Newfoundland. (As it turns out, they are rescue dogs.) I can't blame the dog, really, because with all the gasping for breath, the excessive splashing, and the arms straining over head, my dad's backstroke does sort of look like he's drowning. Called to action, the two-hundred-pound dog dove into the pool to save my dad. In fending off the giant Darth-Vader-looking beast, my dad tore his meniscus. This, of course, was devastating to his golf game, and he would later joke that the damn dog should be put down. I think he was kidding.

■

In the fifth grade, my class created fish tanks out of two-liter soda bottles as a science project. This was every student's favorite part of the whole year because we got to take home the tanks—and our very own goldfish. I dreaded this day for many weeks before, sick to my stomach thinking about having to flush a little translucent body down the toilet after I no doubt did something to kill it. When fish-tank day finally came, I lied and said my parents wouldn't let me have one. Which probably wasn't a lie.

My family's relationship with animals has been historically lukewarm. When approached by someone's dog, I attempt to speak with that syrupy talking-to-a-dog inflection. "There's a big boy!" I'll say, and pat, with four stiff fingers, the top of its head, never quite sure where it wants to be petted.

My mom doesn't even attempt to pet the dog. She instead does a sort of skip-skip-shuffle-step and holds her hands above her head, which everyone knows is the universal canine sign for "Please get up on two legs and jump on me." At which point, she really panics and proceeds to yelp like a dog that would fit inside a purse.

Wild animals are no better. My mom practically aims for them on the road. I should rephrase: She does absolutely nothing to avoid them. She'll defend this by saying, "Well what in the hell'd you want me to do? Swerve and kill us both?"

I have been woken up many a morning to the sound of my mom spraying the deer in the backyard full of beebees. She'll be cloaked in her pink, quilted bathrobe and matching spongy slippers with a pellet gun firm against her shoulder, padding through the yard like Elmer Fudd. "I don't pay for all the teenagers in the neighborhood to come into my kitchen and eat all my food. Why should I be feeding all these deer?" she'll say, tracking a deer that's wandered into her garden for a snack. *POW*. She'll nail one right in the butt. It'll sprint away, its ass flailing wildly in the air. (The bullets aren't strong enough to kill the deer, she's assured me many times, in the same harangue about them spreading Lyme and being over-populated.) "They're a menace to society," she'll say, then swish up the back steps to get her egg casserole out of the oven.

We're not terrible people, I promise. We like humans. We really like humans! Most of the time. And it's not that we dislike animals; we're just not quite sure what to do with them.

Somehow, we used to have a dog. A Welsh corgi named Choo-Choo, because at age two my brother thought she ran like a choo-choo train. We liked Choo-Choo; I swear we did. I even cried when she died. My dad picked me up from my fifth-grade afterschool French class and told me the news. I mustered up some tears because it seemed like the thing to do.

Here comes the bad part: For her fourteen years with our family, Choo-Choo primarily lived outside. While this was an acceptable arrangement when we lived in Georgia, I'm not so sure how humane it was once we moved to Connecticut. "She has a house of her own," my mom would say, motioning toward the door-less, insulation-less wooden shack with three feet of snow on either side. My dad would add, sitting slipper-footed by the fire, "Would you want to live inside this hot house with a fur coat on? I don't think so." I'd look outside as dusk enveloped the miniature wooden igloo, and then back inside at the roaring fireplace, the tartan-plaid blanket draped across the overstuffed sofa, and think to myself, *I'm not so sure.*

It's terrible, I know. Fortunately, it sounds like my mom has turned a corner. "Oh that was just horrible!" she said one day when I mentioned Choo-Choo's living in the cold. My dad, on the other hand, didn't budge. "She had a house!" he said, waving a page of his newspaper wildly. "With blankets!"

■

There are some animals, however, that I sincerely love. I love whales. *The Voyage of the Mimi* was my favorite educational film of all time. It even inspired me to have a *Free Willy*–themed birthday party in the fourth grade. And dinosaurs, I love them. Do they count? I guess I like animals that you can love in a more abstract way.

While I realize furrier animals are inherently cute, fun to cuddle with, and good, loyal companions, they've never really done it for me. Yet I've never understood why it's socially acceptable to openly hate cats, but when I indicate my indifference toward dogs, people look at me like I'm a registered sex offender with a swastika tattooed on my face.

I even saved a cat once. Or saved a party of people from a cat, I should say. (This depends upon whether you were viewing the situation from four legs or two.) A group of us rented a house for a wedding in upstate New York, and we hosted a party after the rehearsal dinner. In a drunken stupor, someone left the front door wide open. In ran a collarless cat, full-speed ahead, weaving through clusters of people and jumping on the furniture. You should have seen how these people reacted. They leapt onto couches, dove onto tabletops, locked themselves in bathrooms. It was as if a chainsaw-wielding, hockey-masked murderer had crashed the party. It's just a cat, people; it's not going to kill you. The cat, no doubt as freaked out as the party guests, retreated to the second floor.

A few minutes later, one of our friends descended to announce, proudly, that he'd solved the problem: He locked the cat in the room with the guy who was passed out. Everyone laughed and seemed to accept this as a suitable solution. Perhaps it was years of latent guilt, my subpar animal affection calling me to arms, but I did not see this as a suitable solution. I put down my Solo cup of vodka-soda and marched up the stairs, opening the bedroom door with the "I've come to save the day" swagger of a male stripper dressed as a fireman. While our human friend was sleeping soundly on the bed, our new feline friend was sprinting in psychotic circles on the floor.

A wave of panic and nausea came over me. I began to have flashbacks from my childhood. The only other time I'd picked

up a cat was during a celebration dance after winning a riv-
eting game of Mall Madness at my friend Veronica's house in
the third grade. The cat seemed nice enough: gray and white
and named Mr. Moe. I scooped him up, hoping he'd partake
in my victory dance, but instead he just bit me on the face.
I tried as best I could to shake the memory from my mind,
crouching down in a coaching-third-base position. If I were
wearing sleeves, I would have rolled them up. I reached down
and squealed as I scooped up the little fur ball. He did not
seem to like this, so I had to hurry down the stairs, his legs
dangling awkwardly below my "this baby's got a dirty diaper"
grip. When we arrived at the front door, I considered tossing
him to see if they really do always land on their feet. But
images of *Free Willy* flashed through my head: Would I throw
a whale at a sidewalk to see if it landed right side up? I don't
think so. Instead, I placed the kitty gently on the front lawn,
pet him affectionately on his creepily small head, and sent him
on his way.

Star Gazing

◼

Throughout all my shifts in the box, I've never seen a celebrity at the hotel, though I am sure they have been there. They are everywhere in LA. That's one thing *Us Weekly* actually has right: Stars are just like us. They really are at the grocery store, and at the gas station, and behind you in line at the bar. (Correction: They are in front of you in line at the bar.) With the box, it's sort of strange to think that, for once, they are looking at me, not the other way around. I'm so accustomed to watching their faces inside boxes, but in the lobby of this hotel, they are forced to watch mine. Well, not forced. I guess they could look at the ground. I am sure they are not particularly impressed. But are they looking? If the box really is a human art installation, as it purports to be, then am I the performer here, and they my audience? The thought is sort of thrilling.

Not-So-Model Behavior

■

The first time I entered the fabled halls of the Condé Nast building—home of *The New Yorker, Vogue,* and *Vanity Fair*— it was not for an interview or a magazine assignment, but to get my picture taken for *Lucky* magazine. Someone knew someone who worked at *Lucky* and thought I would be a good candidate for the magazine's "real people modeling." (Apparently the magazine-slash-shopping-guide features both "models" and "real people." As if the former is not a member of the latter.) It was the summer after my college graduation, and I was living with my parents in Connecticut desperately trying to get an editorial job within those fabled halls. Or anywhere, for that matter. When this peculiar opportunity presented itself to me, I thought, why not? I mean, who doesn't want to be a "real person" for a day?

If nothing else, it was reprieve from my fruitless job search and an excuse to get out of the house. Before the meeting, I spent an embarrassing amount of time orchestrating my outfit. I'd have to wear heels, of course, but I'd wear flats for the walk from the train station. I settled on skinny(ish) jeans—this was 2004, so that version of "skinny jeans" was what would now be called "straight leg"—a loose-fitting tank, and a long, layered necklace that draped to my belly button. My mom dropped me off at the station, and while on the train, I consulted my CoverGirl compact a few too many times.

When I emerged from Grand Central and felt that first subway grate blow its hot breath through my blonde hair, I thought, *This is my Marilyn moment.* Never mind the wet garbage smell. With that, I strutted up East Forty-second, one foot meaningfully placed in front of the other, popping my hips to the side like Tyra had taught me on *Top Model.* I was certain she would think I was fierce.

When I arrived at the famous address—4 Times Square—I hid around a corner to switch my shoes and blot my sweaty face. Once my complexion finally transitioned from dripping to dewy, I popped on my pumps and headed inside. The women in the building were just as I'd imagined: tiny, impeccably dressed, terrifying. I was feeling less model-like by the minute. Why didn't they just cast people from their own lobby? While waiting outside the model booker's office, I thumbed through a copy of *Lucky,* the only magazine they had. A few other women were waiting as well. I tried to figure out if they were models, "real people," or just regular real people. The booker eventually emerged and called my name. She looked startled as I stood. *Oh god,* I thought, *it's that bad? I don't even qualify as a "real person"?* I told her that yes, I was Lilibet, and reached out my hand. "Oh!" she said, shaking it, "I thought you were a real model!" These words nearly knocked me out of my pumps. I tried to mask my elation. "Oh," I said, swatting an imaginary fly in front of me, "I don't know about that."

After quitting track in college, I gained a lot of weight—forty pounds, to be exact—while studying abroad. "I thought the food was bad in London," my friends would say after spending their semesters enjoying crepes in Paris and fettuccini in Florence. "Well," I'd tell them, my inflated arms crossed self-consciously, "Clearly I found plenty to eat." I think, more than anything, my body was in shock. I went from eating like an anemic squirrel and running more than sixty miles a week to spending six months waddling across a pub to fetch another murky stout and a second basket of mayonnaise-covered fries. By that summer after graduation, I had lost most of the weight, but I still didn't feel like a model, and certainly not a "real" one.

Beyond the initial flattery, the model booker was all business. She snapped a few Polaroids: "Look right, look left, hold your hair back with your hand. No not like that, like this. Okay now smile—okay don't smile *that* much." Before I left, I got her card so I could send her a thank you note while casually mentioning I was looking for a job at a magazine.

■

Months later, after moving to California, I thumbed through the stack of business cards I had acquired during my interviews in Manhattan. While I knew most of the magazines didn't have editorial offices in LA, I thought someone might know someone in publishing out here. No one did.

When I tried the booker at *Lucky*, she replied: "So, I don't have any close contacts in magazines out there, but I do know several modeling agencies." I read the email again. Modeling agencies? Was I seeing this right? Even though this woman never used my photo in *Lucky*, she thought I had what it takes to be a model in LA? To have an agent? I checked my reflection in the monitor of Rachel's parents' PC. My skin was tanned and my hair was sun streaked. Most of that college weight was gone. I sucked in my cheeks and puckered my lips. I swished my hair across my shoulders and, with the back of my hand, pushed a half-eaten bowl of ice cream to the edge of the desk. I rolled my shoulders southward and watched as my slouching spine began to unfurl itself, making me three inches taller. I think I might have winked at myself. Flashing a toothpaste-commercial smile at my own reflection, I placed my hands delicately on the keyboard and began composing my reply.

"Thanks so much for getting back to me!" I typed. "I am very interested! Please pass on the necessary details!" I hit send at the top of my Hotmail inbox and watched the email disappear into the abyss. The hairs on my arms stood straighter, too. I crossed my arms and rubbed my hands against my triceps, giving myself a hug. Maybe this wasn't part of the plan. But screw the plan. I was going to be a *model* . . . in *LA*.

The booker at *Lucky* put me in touch with her agent friend, who called me in for a meeting. On the afternoon of the interview, I made a right onto the agency's street—in Beverly Hills, of course. The streets really were lined with palm trees. I craned my head out my window and looked up. They seemed to stretch skyward forever. It looked just like *Troop Beverly Hills*. But where was my Shelly Long mom figure to comfort me and buy me pedicures? The unfamiliarity juxtaposed with the creepy film-set reminiscence made me queasy. What was I doing? A model? In LA? Was this really for me? What would my parents think, having just spent upward of $100K on my college education? I sat in the parking garage and gnawed on my nails. I was early because I had given myself an hour to get there. I drummed my thumbs against the wheel, pulled down the visor, and checked my reflection in the mirror. I licked lipstick from my teeth, and with that, I went into the building.

I told the receptionist I was there for an interview, feeling silly calling it that. Is that what they call it in the modeling world? I wasn't sure. The president of the agency, a friendly former model named Francine, asked me to take a seat in a conference room. Her first words were, "I love your outfit.

You look so cute." She liked my outfit; we were off to a great start. "So tell me a little about yourself," she asked.

"Well, I graduated in May and recently moved out here with some girlfriends." I decided to forgo the business about the writing and the journalism degree. What good would that do anyway? "And I'm really ready to take on something new and exciting." I tried to sit up as straight and skinny as possible on the saggy couch. She asked me a few more questions: where I was from, what part of LA we had moved to, that sort of thing. Then, after only a few minutes, she clasped her hands and said, "Okay, well, I think you're great!"

I was startled. That was it? That was all she needed? No Polaroids, no runway walk, no height, no weight, no measurements? With just a quick look, she was sold. Why had I underestimated myself?

"So," she went on, "your primary responsibilities will be . . ."

Responsibilities? Hmm, I thought. *I wonder what those are? Working out twice a day? Applying Crest Whitestrips? Brushing my hair a lot?*

". . . faxing, filing, answering phones, scanning."

My confusion must have been palpable because she paused. "You do know how to scan, right?"

I tripped over the beginning of at least two sentences. She must have thought I was really scared of scanning. Finally, I stuttered, "No. No, I'm sorry, I actually *don't* know how to scan." My shoulders slumped back to their normal elevation and I cupped my hands together on my lap. "But," I said, wagging a convincing finger in the air, "I am a quick study!"

I think part of me was relieved. While the thought of being a model was flattering, I wasn't sure I had it in me. It seemed like an awful lot of work, staying so skinny. I accepted the job as an assistant at the agency. I would have taken any job at that point; I needed to pay my rent. Even though I was fairly certain I hated LA, I desperately wanted to make the city work, if for no other reason than to prove it to my parents. My poor mom had flown to Boulder after gradu-ation to help pack up my things, which we then boarded onto a U-Haul and drove across eight states to Connecticut. Before I left Boulder, I sold my car—because, I told them, I wouldn't need one in Manhattan. Then, three months later, I announced I was actually not moving to New York, but to California, and they'd have to pay to ship all my belongings *back* across the country. Oh yeah, and could they please buy me a car because I'd need one in LA. I had caused my parents enough anguish already. The least I could do was get a job so they would no longer have to pay my rent. Plus, this woman Francine was pregnant and from New Orleans. Her easy laugh was warm and welcoming and, in the middle of those freakishly unfamiliar surroundings, her southern accent felt like home.

The fact that working at a talent and modeling agency in Beverly Hills enlisted absolutely none of the skills I acquired while getting a writing degree was not lost on me. In addition to various administrative duties, one of my primary responsi-bilities was getting the models to go to their castings, which, I would learn, actually took some skill. It was like herding a pack of underfed, hungover, directionally retarded house cats. (The following year, Rachel got a job at a talent agency, and her boss eventually confessed that it wasn't her education or work experience that got her the position, but the fact that she used to be a camp counselor. "That's just what you need to talk to actors," her boss said.)

From the mouths of models, I have now heard every excuse, explanation, and inane utterance imaginable. Or I should say, unimaginable. You just couldn't make this stuff up. The ex-cuses ranged from the typical "My car won't start" or "I over-slept" to the outrageous "I can't make it to the casting because I burnt my eyeballs in the tanning bed." Were her eyes *open* in the tanning bed? It was a real head scratcher. There were some I had to write down, like the following:

> **Me:** "I'm calling with a casting for you for 2:00 pm tomorrow.
> **Model:** "I can't go on any castings tomorrow."
> **Me:** "Oh. Why not?"
> **Model:** "Because it's a holiday."
> **Me:** "Wait, it is?"
> **Model:** "*Yeah*, Valentine's Day!"
> **Me:** "Well that's not like a real holiday."
> **Model:** "What do you mean?"
> **Me:** "The banks aren't closed, the schools aren't . . . you know what, forget it. Enjoy your day!"

The models often stopped by the office to pick up checks or say hello. They'd roll in, looking effortlessly stunning without a stitch of makeup, sipping iced coffee and smelling of cigarettes. Sometimes, if they didn't have any castings to attend, they'd hang out all day, twirling around in office chairs, regaling us with stories of parties at celebrities' houses in the Hollywood Hills. Some would prattle on while we worked at our desks, trying to ignore them. One day, one of the models announced that she wanted to get a gap put in her teeth.

"Wait. Put *in*?" I asked, swiveling toward her in my desk chair. She was picking something out of her hair.

"Duh," she explained. "Fucked-up teeth are so in right now." (Granted, this was the same girl who once referred to parentheses as "those half-moon thingies.")

Another time, an older client—she had graduated to catalog modeling—fell out of her chair mid-sentence.

"Oh my god, Valerie, are you okay?" I reached for her wrist, its circumference the size of a silver dollar.

"The funny thing," she said as I pulled her back onto the

chair, "is this is the first time I've come into the office sober!" She laughed like a maniac.

"But Valerie, you always come into the office at, like, 11:00 am."

"I know!" she howled. More maniacal laughter.

Successfully relaying audition information to the models was another challenge. This was back when phone calls were still the primary mode of communication and before most cell phones had email access. I'd have to dictate five-digit street addresses—"11317 Ventura Boulevard, Studio City, CA 91604"—over the phone, frequently to someone who was, at that moment, driving, smoking, and petting a small dog in a purse on her passenger seat. Time and time again, while making one of these calls, a model would answer and stop me mid–zip code.

"Wait, will you call back and leave this on my voicemail?" she'd ask.

"Well, I would have left it on your voicemail in the first place if you hadn't picked up," is what I wanted to say. But what I'd really say was, "Sure! No problem!" and then hang up, re-dial, re-recite.

This was also well before iPhones and cars with navigation. This was the era of the *Thomas Guide*, though none of these models owned one. Addresses were often so garbled by bad cell connections that they were totally lost in translation. One afternoon, a model called me in an absolute panic.

"Where the *hell* is this casting?" she demanded, in a whisper.

I repeated the addresses.

"That's where I *am*," she breathily snapped back, "and there is a sign on the door that says NO GUNS ALLOWED."

After some back-and-forth we realized that she thought I had said "Perry Avenue" instead of "Barry Avenue," which landed her right in the middle of the hood. "Okay," I instructed her, now also whispering. "Walk away from the house, get back in your car, and lock the door."

Almost daily, the agency received presents, and most of them were edible. I always thought it was sort of cruel to send your agents cornucopias full of crap you'd never eat yourself. A cookie and muffin combo would arrive from a fancy LA bakery, with a card attached that read: "Thank you for booking me on the Revlon job!" This, from a girl who wouldn't be caught dead eating a muffin. In those first six months, I gained fifteen pounds. I know this because there was a scale in the agency's kitchen. The *kitchen*. It was for weighing the models, but of course we weighed ourselves too, the boxes of See's Chocolates mocking us as we slid the scale tab ever farther to the right.

Aside from babysitting in high school and briefly working as a hostess in college, this was my first job. I didn't yet know that you weren't supposed to eat everything in sight, all the time. Because, I would learn, there was always something to eat. Candy on desks, edible arrangements from clients, cupcakes for a coworker's birthday. The dress code at our office was casual, but for the first few weeks I tried to look cute. By month two, I rarely wore makeup and often showed up with my hair still wet. I made a point of looking like the assistant, not one of the gorgeous models falling out of twirling chairs.

I had accepted my station on the other side of the camera lens. The dream had died. *Lucky* hadn't even used me as a "real person," and the idea of me being a "real model" hadn't crossed Francine's mind. I was simply a real "real person." I could eat all the muffins I wanted.

Worse still, I was surrounded by models at all times, and not just in the office. Because I was the youngest employee, it was my job to accompany the girls to various fancy functions and red-carpet events. The promoters throwing the parties would call our agency and ask for "twelve girls" or "twenty girls" or "our top three" to help up the attractiveness of their events. While I felt lucky to get to attend, in my role as model wrangler/babysitter, I always felt more than a little awkward at these soirees. I was never quite sure what to wear. I felt like a poser donning the same slinky cocktail dresses the real models wore, but jeans and a blazer made me feel frumpy. I was rarely allowed to bring friends to these events, and no guys ever talked to me because I was perpetually engulfed by a pack of perfect tens. I spent the majority of these nights pretending I had to go to the bathroom and looking for Leonardo DiCaprio. (I only found him once, wearing a black leather jacket and a baseball hat, already insulated by his own moat of models.)

I'll never forget one party at "P. Diddy's house." (We later found out that was a rumor started by the event planner. I think they called him "P. Daddy" on the invite so they could get away with it.) At the party was the not-yet-infamous duo—we'll call them Blonde Beard and The Bro—and it took them no time to sniff out our pack of models. The Bro tried to brag to us about how they weren't on the list, and how they had to scale a wall to get into the party, and how he'd ripped his designer pants (I want to say it was an Armani suit). Meanwhile, Blonde Beard told us they were in the process of pitching a reality TV show about their own exploits in Southern California. (Those two have been trying to get famous for a very long time.) Blonde Beard started talking to me, but when I said I was the assistant at the agency that represented all these girls, he quickly lost interest and moved on to the real model to my right. After standing there like an asshole with no one to talk to, I sucked down the rest of my vodka-soda and pretended I had to go to the bathroom.

About a month later, I ran into Blonde Beard at a bar in Hollywood. That night, I wasn't with any models, just real "real people." Again, he tried to strike up a conversation with me.

"We've met," I said.

"Um, *pretty* sure we haven't," he replied.

"Yeah, we met at that fake Puff Daddy party, and you proceeded to totally blow me off when you found out I wasn't a model." I stabbed the lime at the bottom of my glass.

"No wayyyyyyy," he said in his fake surfer drawl. He punched his buddy in the arm to get his attention, then cupped my chin in his hand, asking his friend, "Could I forget a face like this?"

I arched my eyebrows, unconvinced, and retracted my head from his grip. Yet again, I found myself pretending I had to go to the bathroom.

Later that night, Blonde Beard found me and asked for my number. I had no business giving it to him—one, I was dating someone, and two, I never found him remotely attractive. But he was a guy who allegedly only dated models, and he complimented my face.

He called me twice, and twice I didn't answer, guilt-ridden than I'd given him my number in the first place. His first message said, "Lilibet, it's me. Give me a call." Or something like that. The second one said, in the lackadaisical So-Cal cadence that he would later become known for during his horrifying stint on a show that took place in the Hollywood Hills, "Lilibet, what the fuuuuuuuck, why aren't you returning my calls? It's so laaaaaaaaaaaame. Why are you blowing me offffffff?" I was driving west on the 10 when he called. I waited for the last ring, listened to the voicemail, snapped my phone shut, and smiled. I never called him back; the messages were validation enough. If I had only known what a famous freak he would eventually become, I would have held onto those voicemails for dear life.

My other responsibility as a rookie assistant landed me in equally awkward situations. This involved me running the agency's Open Calls, a try-out of sorts for prospective models from three to four on Tuesdays and Thursdays. I'd recite the rundown to hopefuls over the phone: "You must be five foot eight or taller and between the ages of sixteen and twenty-two." And twice a week, girls five foot eight or taller would line the hallways, snapshots of themselves on their laps. I'm not sure why we did this; the agency almost never signed anyone from this human slush pile. I always wanted to—it would have been fun to claim I discovered the next Giselle. But really, more than anything, I just hated saying no. Once, while working the front door of an art gallery party in downtown LA, I unclicked the rope for every single person who showed up, even if they weren't on the guest list. *Especially* if they weren't on the list. I mean, they had come all that way and were so dressed up . . . Unfortunately, the agency's velvet rope was harder to unclick. It is sad to say, but most of these girls had no business believing they were the next Giselle, or even the next girl in the JCPenney circular. I just couldn't bring myself to break that news, so instead I'd say, with the *hey-girlfriend* inflection of Tyra Banks, "You're a beautiful girl, Chastity, but you're just not right for this agency. I would definitely try your luck somewhere else, though." And with that, they'd gather up their snapshots and head down the road to Elite.

It was the same dodge-and-flatter dance, week after week, until the afternoon Amanda walked in. Amanda, a statuesque African American woman with incredible calves. Was this the next Naomi Campbell?

"Welcome! Please, take a seat," I said. She gave her skirt a tug as she crossed her long legs. "So, what's your name?"

"Amanda," she said. Her voice was reminiscent of something I couldn't quite place. It was rich, velvety, vixen-esque.

"Great, Amanda, tell me a little about yourself." With that, Amanda placed her hand on my knee and looked me sternly in the eye. Okay, I thought, this was a first. Clearly this Amanda had the boldness it takes to make it in the modeling world. With her hand still on my knee, she headlocked me in eye contact and restated her name, this time dragging out the syllables:

"A-Man-Duh."

"Right, Amanda, you said that," I said.

"A man," she paused. What the hell? Why did she keep repeating her name? And would she please remove her hand from my thigh? She cocked her head at me and batted her false lashes. And then—welcome, Lilibet, welcome—I finally made it to the party. Her Adam's apple appeared as she pronounced the last syllable, "Duh."

Fortunately, scenarios as such provided endless amounts of amusement for the agency's employees. I loved my coworker's like dysfunctional family members, and we spent a decent portion of our days doubled-over in our ergonomically correct office chairs. You just don't get diversions like Amanda the cross-dressing model in every place of employment. Some of the characters who worked in the office were as ridiculous as those we represented. The guy who sat across from me, Dave, took it upon himself to initiate "Jersey Fridays." Sort of like "Hat Day" in middle school. On Fridays, he told us, we were allowed to wear our favorite team jersey to work. I am still not entirely sure how this Dave ended up working at a modeling agency, an industry entirely dominated by women and gay men, neither of whom would be caught dead wearing a jersey to work. (Two of the male model agents, both of them flamboyant and overweight, used to bicker like Dorothy and Rose on *The Golden Girls*. When one announced he'd lost ten pounds, the other said, "Oh *please*. That's like throwing a deck chair off the Titanic.")

It goes without saying that "Jersey Fridays" never caught on, except with its founder. Every Friday, without fail, Dave was clad in one of the following: a boxy mesh Cleveland Browns NFL jersey; a snug, University of Arizona college basketball jersey, which he wore over a tee; or a cotton jersey-esque Mets T-shirt. (Dave was an equal-opportunity fan, not partial to one particular region of the country.) Dave also occasionally brought his cat to the office, stroking it on his lap while he worked. The giant fluff ball, covered in snowy fur, would poke out from under his desk, right on top of his crotch. My favorite thing about Dave, however, was not the cats or the Cleveland Browns, but the fact that he would take his lunch breaks in the office, and he would take them *very* seriously. If I tried to get his attention during this designated hour, he'd wave his hand frantically in my face—"I'm at lunch! I'm not here! You don't see me!"—and continue walking down the hall.

In the year and a half I worked at the agency, we moved offices three times. While each office was different, one thing remained the same: the towering wall of "comp cards"—glossy paper rectangles, each with a close-up of a model on the front and four smaller pictures of her on the back. All day long, a hundred beautiful faces would stare at us, each with the same pissed-off expression. Across the bottom of the cards were the model's names and heights. They all went by their first names, some sexy and foreign-sounding (Oksana, Michiko, Katarina), others Southern-California-cute (Ashley, Chelsea, Desiree). If there was any overlap, we added a surname initial, like on *The Bachelor*. The clients called them by their first name and last initial as well—heaven forbid they book the busty blonde "Caroline B." for the Chloe job, when what they really wanted was the waifish, brown-haired "Caroline M."

Because I'm a borderline hoarder, I still have my notebooks from this job. Based on one entry, it appears I was trying to keep the models straight. I had jotted down a handful of models' names and some identifying triggers to help me remember them. Next to the name "Jamie" it says: "Gave directions, wavy brown," and next to the name "Nina" it says: "Nice, red hair." (I'm not sure which was nice: Nina or her hair.) Apparently "Megan" was a golfer because I wrote: "Megan: Blonde, golf, very nice," while "Amber" gave me less to work with. For her it just says, "Curly blonde." It seems redundant that I noted "Yalia" was "foreign." In what is by far my favorite descriptor, next to the name "Sarah," it simply says: "Dated Leo." Enough said. I clearly wasn't going to forget her.

When I wasn't making notes about the models, I was handling pictures of their perfectly proportioned faces. Francine wasn't kidding about the scanning; my newly acquired skill took up a large part of my workday. Back then, model agencies re-touched photographs the old fashioned way: someone actually painted over imperfections on large matte photographs, concealing under-eye circles and flyaway hairs. After that, it was my job to scan the now-flawless image back into the computer. We also took Polaroids the old-fashioned way, meaning we took real Polaroids. (They still call it "taking Polaroids," but they take the pictures with a digital camera.) I'd ask a girl to come in "with clean hair and face" and have her pose next to a window. If a client needed swimsuit Polaroids, there was a spare bikini in the bathroom. Like the woman at *Lucky*, I instructed the girls to look right, look left, face forward, smile.

Doing this, of course, reminded me of that day at *Lucky* and of my circuitous route into the modeling agent world. Although I had absolutely no interest in moving up in this industry, I had somehow stayed for almost two years.

The Polaroids required scanning as well. I'd tape four Polaroids to a piece of 8 x 11 printer paper and write the model's name and height across the bottom of the page with a Sharpie. Then, hunched over the scanner, I'd upload the images. I did this over and over, all day long, which was both incredibly monotonous and crushingly depressing. I wasn't depressed because I wasn't a model, though I often coveted their wasp-like waists and angular faces (my cheekbones had vanished months before). I just wanted to do something with my life that I had even a vague interest in. If I wasn't tracking down a model's UGGs in some wardrobe trailer, I was booking their hair appointments at Frédéric Fekkai, making their travel arrangements for a swimwear shoot in Bora Bora, or dictating directions to a famous director's house in the Pacific Palisades. My job was a relentless reminder that, while I was very busy making other girls' lives more fabulous—girls who were my exact same age, no less—my life was standing still.

■

I knew my last day at the agency was inevitable when I returned from lunch one afternoon to find the final straw on my desk. It was in the form of a Post-it note, stuck to my computer screen. I peeled it from the monitor while hooking my purse to the back of my chair. I remained standing while I read it, trying to process the implications: "Morgan H. needs a bikini wax." *This must be some sort of inside joke,* I thought. Maybe I accidentally snapped an unfortunate Polaroid of Morgan H. revealing an unkempt nether region?

"Dave, did you write this?" I asked.

Dave responded, not looking up from his computer, "She said Tuesday or Wednesday after ten would be good."

"I'm sorry, I am supposed to *schedule* her bikini wax?" I asked.

"Yeah," Dave answered, unfazed. "She needs it done before the Quicksilver shoot."

I sat down at my desk and laid my forehead on top of my keyboard until it started to beep. This was too much. While it was one thing to schedule haircuts and highlights for these girls, it was quite another to make appointments for the removal of their pubic hair. I had to get out. While I loved my colleagues, this job was slowly but surely killing my soul.

It was already easy enough to become invisible in LA, spending most of my time behind the windshield of my car with fast food on my lap. While I wouldn't be caught dead walking down Madison Avenue with a milkshake in hand, I had absolutely no problem driving down Wilshire Boulevard, sucking an Oreo McFlurry through a straw. Behind the anonymous screen of that squawking drive-through speaker,

I had no issue boldly proclaiming, "You know what, make it a large." Like a true friend, Rachel finally intervened. "Maybe you should switch to frozen coffee drinks," she suggested.

That "real person" who strutted up Forty-second street like she owned the goddamn place was now buried under fifteen pounds of fast food milkshakes and two years of stroking other people's egos. "You have *amazing* eyes," I'd say to one of our models. "And those legs!" I'd also turned into the type of person who thinks it's appropriate to wear a hoody sweat-shirt to work.

In high school, my girlfriends and I would often say, "Stella's gotta get her groove back." Why the title of an all-black comedy about middle-aged women became the mantra of our teenage lives, I did not know. All I knew was, *this* Stella needed to get her groove back.

I gave Francine my two-weeks notice, and, just like Shelly Long, she could not have been more supportive. She knew I wasn't long for this world. Francine helped plan a going-away party on my last day of work, which landed on a Jersey Friday. It was supposed to be a civilized, drop-by-the-office-around-six-for-wine-and-cheese affair. We invited all the models, and many of them came, some bearing gifts. (I had legitimately become friends with a few of them.) One of the models (the red-headed and, it turned out, very nice "Nina") gave me a Def Leppard CD and a bottle of Patrón. That gift, we decided, needed to be opened immediately. Within minutes, the low-key affair turned into, well, whatever you get when you mix a bunch of under-weight models, tequila, and hair metal. People were dancing on the desks, and at some point, I initiated a rolling-desk-chair race. As I waited for a cab to pick me up (my car stayed there until the morning), I nudged Dave to tell him the party was over. He was passed out, facedown on his desk. For unknown reasons, his shirt was off, and a backpack was strapped to his back. His Mets T-shirt was in a heap beside his chair.

Paper Planes

▪

Every month there is a new installation in the box, each conceptualized by a different artist. Sometimes the back wall is covered in a collage of Polaroids. Sometimes it's painted in bold, modern stripes. Sometimes it pulses with Dan Flavin-esque neon lights. While some installations are quite pleasant to be a part of—a tranquil surf video projected behind me, say—others are more unnerving.

For a month, green paper lanterns and pink plastic flowers of an undeterminable variety hung from the ceiling of the box. I couldn't sit up without one of them hitting me on the head. While that was annoying, it was actually the least troubling part of the installation. Behind me, on the wall, were pictures of odd little dolls in poses that failed to be cute: at the beach, in a rose garden, in a wedding dress, peering over a sunflower. The worst was a picture of one doll holding a smaller, even creepier doll. No matter what these dolls were up to, their expressions remained unchanged: foreheads too large for their faces, eyes of alien proportions. Dozens of bug-eyes fixed on me, for seven hours straight.

Some installations are three-dimensional to the point of interactive. These can be a bit of a nuisance. Once, the box was filled with dozens of paper airplanes, all different shapes and sizes, hung at various heights from the ceiling by fishing line. The creator of this installation had asked that the fan be left on to create the effect that the airplanes were flying. While I'm sure this was a dazzling display to see from the safety of the lobby, it was a shitstorm to be stuck inside—a million adorable airplanes swirling and loop-de-looping their pointy little noses right into my face. After pulling one too many out of my hair, which was whipped into a beehive at this point, I decided my safest option was to hunker down as close to the mattress as possible, in the no-fly zone.

I Am a Slash

People often feel compelled to offer their unsolicited opinions about Los Angeles. One time, at a cocktail party with my mom on the East Coast, a woman in her early forties said, "Oh I *hate* LA," with the kind of disdain that is typically reserved for a colonoscopy. This is where I live. Where I *chose* to live. This is my home. If someone tells me they've taken up residence in even some of my least favorite cities—New Haven, Connecticut, for example—I'll search for something redeeming to say, like, "*Amazing* pizza. You've *got* to go to Peppy's."

Before I moved, the Southern California commentary was relentless. "The smog is awful," was a common thread. "Aren't the people very fake?" was another, typically from women. The most common criticism was, of course, about the traffic, typically from someone who had never been to LA. The critic's closing remarks were normally along the lines of, "Why are you moving there again?"

Soon after I moved, I realized that people who live in LA loved talking about traffic, too. It's like Midwesterners and weather, or Southerners and humidity.

"It was an absolute goddamned nightmare getting down Olympic this afternoon," Melissa would say, grabbing desperately for a happy hour menu.

"Sunset was jammed all the way to the 405," Rachel would add, sucking a glass of half-priced sangria through a straw.

The *Saturday Night Live* skit "The Californians" is not hyperbole. The freeways all take a "the" before their number. I once instructed a friend who had recently moved here, "Just take The 10 to The 110 to The 101 North," with no sense of irony at all. She thought I was quoting *SNL*. In actuality, I was just trying to get her back to Silverlake.

The bad traffic, I would learn, was one of those LA stereotypes that would prove to be true. Like the freeways being much less congested on Jewish holidays, it was just fact. And there was traffic at all hours of the day; the roads could be just as busy at one o'clock on a Wednesday as five o'clock on a Friday or noon on a Saturday. There was no method to the madness. After a few weeks of enduring traffic jams that looked like a scene from the "Everybody Hurts" music video (and contemplating getting out of the car and walking, or lying down in the carpool lane), it occurred to me that traffic patterns didn't follow the conventional formula in LA because no one, as far as I could tell, had a job.

In this city that centered around the entertainment industry, everyone buzzed in a million different directions, like panicked planets orbiting the sun. It was agents going to meetings, casting directors getting to callbacks, producers trying to make it to set by six. And those were just the people with full-time jobs. A bizarrely disproportionate percentage of the population seemed to be composed of freelance somethings: freelance producers, freelance set designers, freelance makeup artists, and so on and so forth. Many people seemed to be many things all at once. A line from *Lonesome Jim* came to mind while I was sitting in traffic: "I'm a writer. And a dog walker. And I work part-time at an Applebee's." I remember thinking, *What is wrong with these people?*

Yet, after two years, I quit my proper full-time job at the talent agency because I wanted to write. I scoured the editorial landscape in LA and took an internship at *Flaunt,* an independent arts and fashion magazine. I called my dad and told him my plan. I was going to intern during the day—get contacts, experience, clips—and work at a restaurant at night to pay my rent.

"Have you run the numbers?" he asked, sounding none too thrilled. I looked down at the notepad where I had scribbled a list of my monthly expenses: rent, utilities, car insurance, food.

"It will work," I said, even though I knew damn well it wouldn't. In fact, while interning at the magazine, I accrued an impressive (horrifying) amount of debt on a now-closed credit card.

Even so, I loved it at *Flaunt.* In addition to housing a stable of extraordinarily talented writers, photographers, and designers, the magazine was known for throwing some of the most legendary parties in LA. The editor-in-chief was a fiery, five-foot-five Venezuelan man named Luis. His husband, Jim, was the art director. With a tanning-booth tan and black lacquered hair, Luis looked like he was made of wax. If the devil wore Prada at *Runway,* then the devil wore John Varvatos jeans and Chrome Hearts jewelry at *Flaunt.* Except that he was far from the devil, more like your favorite flamboyant uncle. He was hilarious and generous and kind, if not a little bit insane.

Everyone was a little bit insane there—it was just the sort of chaos I had been craving. Dogs darted down the hallways, an unnamed cat lived in an upstairs closet, and everyone smoked cigarettes out of their office windows. Forget a scale in the kitchen or spare bikinis in the bathroom, more often than not, there was no toilet paper to be found. During my interview, the guy asking me questions was wearing high-top Converse and a pair of long johns under a pair of shorts. His wiry hair was pulled into an unkempt bun, and he would later show me, with pride, the "booger wall" next to his desk. The offices were smack in the center of Hollywood, on a traffic-choked street just south of Sunset Boulevard. I finally knew what Phyllis Diller meant when she said, "Living in Hollywood is like living in a lit cigarette butt." But that, too, only added to the office's filthy, fabulous, fraternal appeal.

Yet after a year, I told them it was time for me to quit. I don't know why I left. I probably should have stayed and asked them to give me a full-time position. Afterward, they told me they would have; all I had to do was ask. So taken by the free-flowing lifestyles of all the freelancers that surrounded me, I think I was scared of something so full-time. Thus, I made up my mind: I was going out on my own to become a freelance writer. In my deluded, twenty-four-year-old mind, I thought I could make a living doing this.

Before I knew it, I had become one of those people who populated the freeway at midday; who thought it was just as normal to throw a birthday party on a Wednesday as it was on a Saturday; one of those work-from-homers who took up all the treadmills at the gym at two o'clock and were always talking about what project they were working on, though there were probably no projects at all.

One day, soon after taking that terrifying, paycheck-less leap, a girlfriend called on her lunch break. She worked in finance in San Francisco. I raced to pick up before the last ring and said breathlessly, wrapped in a towel, "Hi, so sorry, I just got out of the shower."

"What do you mean you just got out of the shower?"

"What do you mean what do I mean I just got out of the shower?"

"It's two o'clock on a Tuesday."

And that's when it hit me: I was, officially, unapologetically, *one of them*.

Little did I know my timing for this transition could not have been worse. Within months, the bottom dropped out of not only the publishing industry, but the entire economy. Everyone in magazines was terrified of the Internet. "It's the end of print," they'd say. Many publications shuttered, and those that didn't desperately strained to keep their pages above water. Magazines that used to pay me a dollar a word dropped that to ten cents, or in some cases, to nothing. During this period, I got an assignment from a small but reputable arts magazine to write a 500-word piece about a young, up-and-coming director. I emailed the editor-in-chief to ask how much they were going to pay me. He responded: $50. I wrote back, "Fifty dollars, how about a hundred?" He replied, almost immediately, "No!!" There were really two exclamation points.

The glamour of this bohemian, work-from-home lifestyle quickly lost its luster when I completely ran out of money. Suddenly, my salon-purchased shampoos were replaced by bottles that said "Compare to." I started washing my car—not just the windshield, but the entire vehicle—with a squeegee at the gas station. This, because I couldn't afford a car wash. Car washes are nine dollars.

When I'd tell someone I was a writer in LA, more often than not they'd want to know about my screenplay. When I'd reply, "No, actually, I write for magazines," they'd say, "Oh! Like movie reviews?" (This was part of an actual conversation, though the woman who said this also asked who "does" my eyelashes. Um, *I* do.) I realized the only way to stay afloat as a writer in LA at the height of the recession was to supplement that job with, oh, about a million others.

That's when I turned into a full-blown "slash": a writer/editor/actress/model/waitress/etc. I was a living, breathing, beverage-slinging, audition-going, electricity-being-cut-off, LA cliché. My slashiness was indiscriminating and far-reaching. I was a cocktail waitress, a leg model, a tray-passer at parties. I was an extra in a Smirnoff Ice commercial. I was a dead person in a music video. One time, the right side of my face was on an episode of *Entourage*. In one particularly misguided moment of weakness, I volunteered to be a "hair model" and had all of my long blonde hair chopped off for $250 and a couple of bottles of deep conditioner. And, I became a Box Girl.

When I told my parents about the box, they were, understandably, a little confused. "You're going to do what? Where? Huh?" My liberal-minded mom was more accepting of the idea as she is very into contemporary art. My dad, on the other hand, has a hard time comprehending any job that doesn't involve stock options and a 401K. He is a man who reads *Forbes* and watches CNBC from market open to market close. He once suggested I sue "those bastards" at The University of Colorado for giving me a degree in something that can't make me any money. Then he added that he used to make more money while going to the bathroom than I had made in the last year. To this day, he still doesn't know what the Box Girl "uniform" entailed. I think I told him "white pajamas."

My dad believes you go to college and get a job. "A real one." He doesn't understand how his daughter could be carrying a $900 Bottega Veneta bag (my mom's old one) while declining a side of guacamole at Chipotle because it was an additional two dollars. "Champagne taste on a beer budget," he liked to say.

And yes, my parents could have supported me. But I didn't want them to. That's not to say there wasn't a significant safety net; my dad bailed me out of many a financial clusterfuck over the years. But for the most part, I tried my pitiful best to get by on my own. My parents paid for my college education, in full. The least I could do was go out and make stupid decisions all on my own.

Run Lilibet Run

About a year after I left the modeling agency, my direct boss, Pam, suggested I go on commercial auditions. Actually, I am not entirely sure this is true. I think *I* might have suggested that I go on commercial auditions. It's just so much less embarrassing to say it was her idea. They weren't going to send me down the runway at Chanel, but perhaps on the occasional audition for a Colgate commercial. At the time, I was interning at one magazine, freelancing for others, and cocktailing at a restaurant. I thought booking the occasional commercial would be a great way to bring in some extra money. Little did I know that "booking the occasional commercial" is about as easy as "buying the winning Powerball ticket at your local 7-Eleven." But by sneaking in the back door, I became a commercial actress, and the assistant who replaced me had to leave me messages spelling out five-digit street addresses for casting facilities in Burbank. I did, however, schedule my own bikini waxes.

The only commercials I ever actually booked were for running- or fitness-related ads, and that's because with all this newfound freelancer time on my hands, I was running many miles most days. That, and the fact that the other actresses interpreted "Come to the audition in running attire" to mean, "Show up smelling like cigarettes in yoga pants and flip-flops." The art director for an Asics campaign said he knew he was going to book me as soon as I got out of my car.

"You had on running shoes," he said. "And your hair was in a ponytail."

The bar was set pretty low.

My success in the commercial realm has been modest at best, mortifying at worst. While I have made a fool out of myself in front of very good-looking strangers at more than one audition, one such experience will forever hold the title of Most Embarrassing Audition Ever.

A friend of mine was producing an Old Navy commercial, so she asked me to come straight to the "callbacks." Meaning, I jumped over a hundred girls and got to audition with only a handful of finalists. Because fitness commercials were the only ones I had ever come remotely close to booking, I assumed this was a callback for Old Navy's fitness line. Thus, I interpreted the wardrobe instructions of "short shorts and a tank top" to mean "running shorts and a running tank top."

As soon as I walked into the casting facility, I knew something had gone horribly wrong. The other women were dressed in short denim cut-offs, heels, and slinky little tank tops. They were all models—*real* models—with long legs and thick, flowing hair, which had been curled into perfect ripples that spilled over their shoulders. They turned to look when I arrived. I stood at the entrance, my thin hair strung into a ponytail, my chest flattened into a sports bra, wearing shorts with built-in underwear. Standing there, I wondered if they'd notice if I just started walking backward out the door.

Immediately, my producer-friend spotted me, and I was stuck. "No, you look great," she said when I questioned my attire. "I live five minutes away," I said. "I can go change." She insisted that I looked perfect in what I had on. She was trying to be sweet. I really wish she hadn't been.

As I filled out my information in the waiting room, I plotted my attack: *When I go into the audition room, I'll make some joke about my outfit. I'll make them laugh. It will all be fine.* Moments later, a casting assistant came out and said the creative team was ready for us. Us? We had to all go in together? I should have just sprinted out the door. I was wearing running shoes. My friend grabbed my arm and said, "Let's go, hot stuff." At this point I was fairly certain she was just messing with me.

Twelve of us marched in—them, statuesque in their stilettos, me, squatty in my tennis shoes—and took our positions, side-by-side, along a line of masking tape stuck to the floor. These women were standing in the most stunning positions, arrangements I would have never even thought of: chin up, shoulders back, chest forward, one sinewy arm resting gingerly on right hip, pelvis thrust forward, left foot pointed ever so slightly to the southwest. I looked to my right, then to my left: They were all doing it, in lock step, as if preparing to bring their knees to their chests in a Rockettes-style cancan.

I shifted my weight in my extra-stability running shoes and put my hands on my hips. *Wait, that's too many hands,* I thought. *I look like a cheerleading coach. Only one hand.* I dropped one arm and raised my shoulders to my ears. ("Don't wear your shoulders like earrings," I could hear my mom saying.) *Shit.* I tipped my nose toward the ceiling and looked out of the corners of my eyes to make sure I was doing it right. I wasn't. I looked like an asshole.

We were told to slate our names for the camera, which basically—I had always thought from working at the agency—just meant saying your name. Apparently not. These girls had moves I'd never seen before: say name (with enthusiasm!), rotate right, rotate left, complete a full turn, flip hair, look back toward camera, do sexy/pouty face, then flash a big smile and say name again (this time with a more resonating, sexy sound to it). I was screwed. There was no way I could remember all those steps.

But if there was anything I did have in my arsenal that just screamed Old Navy, it was large, straight, white teeth. I've never had braces, and I've been told my teeth look like the ones that sit on the dentist receptionist's desk. I apply Crest Whitestrips religiously, if for no other reason than it is one of my many ritualistic procrastinations from writing.

When it was my time to "slate," I said my first and last name (which I sincerely have a hard time pronouncing) and did a quick twirl in my sneakers. This was not executed as delicately as I had hoped. The tennis-shoe twirl made that terrible, running-suicides-on-the-basketball-court screeching noise. In an attempt to recover, I flashed the most gigantic smile I could muster. This, no doubt, did not read "Old Navy," but rather, "borderline personality disorder."

The camera operator explained the premise of the commercial. Mr. T—yes, as in *The A-Team*—was also starring in the commercial, and he would be manning a "T-Machine": a magical apparatus that transforms boxy T-shirts into form-fitting ones. "From boxy to foxy!" the art director chimed in. The camera operator told us to walk "as if on a runway" to the corner of the room, and, at the end of the imaginary catwalk, act as if our ill-fitting T-shirts had been magically reincarnated into sexy little tops.

This had gone from bad to worse. The twirl was embarrassing enough. Now I had to strut along an imaginary catwalk in an ensemble better suited for pushing a jogging stroller? It's hard to be sexy in a pair of tennis shoes. I have a newfound respect for that girl in the Shape-Ups commercial.

These models' slates were just the beginning. During the actual audition, they strutted their stuff like it was fashion week in Milan. They had the flouncy stride, the hip pop, the tossed-back smile/laugh at the turn, the swooshy walk back with the sexy, over-the-shoulder grin at the end. While waiting my turn, I considered my options. I could just walk out. No, speed walk out. My purse was on the other side of the room, though. I'd have to cross in front of the current auditioner and pass the camera. I'd probably trip over some vital cords and take the whole apparatus down with me. Not a good idea. Maybe I could just pretend to pass out? But that's almost more embarrassing. I was suddenly snapped into action when someone called, "Next!"

The only close cousin to the runway walk while wearing sneakers is the power walk. So I stalked along the imaginary runway, swinging my arms beside me like a middle-aged mom summiting a neighborhood hill. When I reached the end, it was time to engage in some T-shirt transformation theatrics. I had no idea what to do. I tugged on my imaginary ill-fitting top (which, in my case, wasn't imaginary) and made a frowny face. Then (god this is so hard to write) I held my hands in front of my shirt and did "spirit fingers," twinkling my digits as if they harnessed the magical power of the T-Machine. I then opened my hands so my palms faced up as if to say, "Voilà," like the ladies on *The Price Is Right* do after revealing what's behind door number four. Finally, I did the only other thing I knew to do: flashed my giant, crazy-person smile. I looked at my friend, who was looking at her feet—and suppressing a great deal of laughter.

When I returned to my place in the line-up, I waited for the final few girls to complete their turns. I marveled at their unsqueaky twirls, their poise, their appropriate wardrobe selection. After everyone was done, the art director stood and thanked all of us for coming in. He then told us they would get in touch with our agents, and we were free to leave. Most of the models took their time leaving the casting room, some swinging by the director's chair to say a personal thank you for letting them audition. I power-walked to retrieve my purse, taking care to avoid eye contact with anyone in the room. With my bag firmly wedged under my now-sweaty armpit, I was finally able to enlist my ensemble for its proper use—and sprinted to my car.

Like Visiting Day in Jail

■

My Blackberry *de-dinks*. It's a text from my college friend Dave who is in LA for work. He says he and our other friend Matt are coming to see me. To see what this box is all about.

I'm excited about this. In three years, no one has ever come to see me in the box, though everyone always talks about how they want to come. This is probably because the majority of my friends live either by the beach or in the eastern neighborhoods of LA, both of which are only five to fifteen miles away but, with LA traffic, can be an hour-plus trip. It is noteworthy that my first friends to visit me at The Standard live in New York, a six-hour flight away.

I'm on the phone when I look up and see them standing at the front desk. They are leaning on the counter, pretending to be on their phones, pretending not to notice me. I scream and wave, which is not allowed, but I can't help myself. Fortunately, the concierge is too focused on Facebook to notice. I hang up and call Dave's phone while they sit on a couch in the lobby and pass it back and forth. We joke that it's like visiting day in jail. Dave asks if he would get in trouble if he pressed his lips against the glass and gasped, "I'll wait for you!" like they do in the movies.

The only other person who's ever recognized me while I was in the box was the art director at another LA magazine I had written for. He sometimes deejayed at the bar at The Standard. My Blackberry buzzed, "Lilibet, is that you in the box?" My eyes shot up. I scanned the lobby. I couldn't find him. I wrote back, "Yes it's me in here! Where are you?" But by that time, he was out of sight, already in the bar, tucked into the deejay booth.

Dear Mr. Retoucher

Pam said I needed professional headshots. I had plenty of friends who were very handy with a camera, but she wasn't having it, so I made an appointment with a photographer named Brian. Brian took photos at his house, in his backyard. There was a female assistant there, too. She didn't do much but make me feel slightly better about not getting raped or kidnapped by this complete stranger who had lured me into his house with the promise of "making me look beautiful."

I did three different "looks," which I knew from working on the other side of the lens meant "outfits." I insisted on doing my own hair and makeup for the shoot, which ended up being a bad idea. As it turns out, professional cameras and midday backyard lighting are not the most forgiving.

When I got the pictures back, it was a mess of flyaway hairs, uneven skin tone, and dark circles under my eyes. As a pretty photogenic person, I was horrified by the results. How was I going to get any auditions with these disasters?

I immediately called a girlfriend who was an actress.

"I hate them," I said. "I look like Charlize Theron in *Monster*."

"There is no way you look like Charlize Theron in *Monster*," she said.

"Yes, there is," I said.

"Just get them retouched, they'll be fine."

Retouching. Genius.

After sending the pictures to Pam, she agreed with the retouching idea. (I didn't press her for specifics.) I emailed the three photos I hated the least to a photography lab in Hollywood, along with the following instructions:

Hi, please see attached jpegs for retouching.[4]

For the first image, "Lilibet Photo 1," please touch up the lines around my eyes and even out the skin tone. Can you whiten the whites of my eyes? If so, please do so, they look a little blood shot.

For the second image, "Lilibet 2," please fix the flyaway hair, and can you make the lips a touch (just a touch) pinker? Or redder—just a bit more color?? Not sure if you can do that.

Lastly, for the third image, can you remove the zit to the right of my mouth, and clean up the lines around my eyes? Also, if you can, could you make my teeth a bit whiter? And, again, if possible, give my lips a TINY bit more color??

Please email me back to let me know if this is possible and also to give me a quote on price and how long this will take.

THANKS

Lilibet.

After clicking on my Sent Mail tab to make sure the attachments went through, I reread the message. It was sort of horrifying. Could I have been any more nitpicky? Why didn't

---

4 This was the actual email.

I just tell them to give me a new nose and a new set of boobs while I was at it? Maybe highlight my hair and shave off a few extra pounds? Had I become like the image-obsessed girls I used to represent? Freaking out over a few fine lines and flyaway hairs?

What had gotten into me? Who asks someone to pretty much renovate her entire face with a digital paintbrush? I wanted to write him back, to explain I really wasn't like this, I promised. *I don't even wear makeup most days! I'm wearing sweatpants as I type this! I don't even own an eyelash curler!* (But that's just because they scare me.)

But the retoucher responded before I could write him back:

Hi Libet[5] thank you for inquire with us[6]

the price for image #1-2 are $35.00 each and for image #3 is $55.00

Huh. As it turned out, Ronnie the Retoucher was totally unfazed. Of course he was; this is Hollywood. He was more than used to this kind of thing. Plus, the fact that English appeared not to be his first language made me feel less embarrassed. It was like getting a bikini wax from an Eastern European woman as opposed to an American; in some abstract way, the language barrier created some distance.

I was relieved. The truth was, I did care how these came out. I did not want to look like Charlize Theron in *Monster*. I wanted to look good. After spending two years surrounded by models, playing frumpy to their fetching, this was hard to embrace.

---

5 Yes, he misspelled my name, even though the correct spelling was right there in my email address.

6 Also the actual email.

Metamorphosis

■

Tonight, about an hour into my shift in the box, somewhere in the space between reading and online window-shopping, I decide I want to find out who came up with this concept. I email a woman in The Standard's design department, and she writes back, promptly, "I'm sorry but we don't give out background information on design details or concepts at the hotels to anyone, including press. André and his design team came up with the concept for each of the hotels."

I search "André" and "The Standard." André Balazs. He owns several hotels and, according to Wikipedia, went to Cornell and Columbia. And, according to Google, he's dated Uma Thurman and Chelsea Handler, among others. But I'm not really interested in that. I'm interested only in this: He is a man. Of *course* he is a man. This manufactured reality could only be hatched from the head of a man. Men like to think that women lie around on their living room floors wearing itty-bitty white shorts and tiny white tank tops, always looking pretty, never making a mess.

If this André actually saw me at home he would see someone Swiffering her floor and picking at the pores on her face.

But that is a luxury of being a Box Girl. I get to transform. One moment I'm a writer in a bleach-stained shirt, the next moment I'm slithering across a mattress in short white shorts. Standing next to the box before my shift, molting my clothes— my sweater with the holes in the elbows, my jeans that smell like mildew—I get to slough off *that* me. I get to become *another* me: *blonde me, tall me, long-legged me.*

Out There

A girl reads a book on a couch in the corner of the lobby. She bites the skin on the side of her nails while she does this and has checked her phone three times in the last minute.

A guy waits for his car, wearing tight, citrus-colored jeans, rolled at the ankles. His black hair is slick on the sides and is spiked into a shark's fin. With the boat shoes and striped tank top, his look is sort of Hollywood-meets-The-Hamptons.

Three British women walk beside a bellhop who is pushing their luggage—seven suitcases total. "I slept well, but I'm still quite tired," one of them says.

A girl, about my age, walks toward the box with her parents. Her dad is wearing a baseball hat and a zip-up jacket. He looks like a Classic Dad-dad, like someone who orders a lot of stuff from L.L.Bean. Her mom is wearing an Hermès scarf under a blazer and expensive-looking flats. The daughter points at me, and I quickly look down. "This is the thing I was talking about," she says.

I am constantly watching the people in the lobby, wondering where they are coming from, why they are here, how long they'll stay. I make assumptions about them, pass judgments on them, silently criticize their wardrobe selections. All the while, I know they are doing the same to me. It's strange because, in a lot of ways, being in the box is like being a writer. It isolates me and, at the same time, puts me on display. When me and my writing, or me and my thighs, feel like coming out of our little cave, all of my vulnerabilities are out there for the public to pick apart.

I Am Not a Beagle

Tonight the box is filled with dozens of colored balls that illuminate if you toss them. It's like the ball pit at Chuck E. Cheese's, minus the pee smell. I've carved out an area for my myself and my computer.

The door opens. It's the concierge. *Oh no, not again. Do I have too much stuff in here? How could he even tell with all these balls?*

"Hey, could you throw the balls around a little bit? Make them light up? That's the point of the installation." I cock my head sideways and scrunch my eyebrows at him. He cannot be serious.

He appears to be serious.

"Oh, okay, sorry," I say, and spike a royal blue ball against the mattress.

"Awesome," he says, and shuts me back in.

But I don't want to sit here and toss a ball around for seven hours. If that's the aesthetic they're going for, they should have hired a beagle. I wiggle back down to my laptop, slithering through a sea of balls on my stomach, plying them out from under me as I go. A minute later, I retract my right knee and forcefully release it, sending a flurry of balls flying, the box ablaze in all their glory.

Only The Lonely

If this is hard to believe, I assure you, it's even harder to admit: One time I cried in the box. And here's the most embarrassing part: It was on Valentine's Day.

That night, the back wall was painted in bright asylum white and scored with three thick black lines that stretched the length of the box. On top of each line was a series of white tiles with one block letter drawn on each in an art-deco font. A dotted string of lights illuminated the letters from below, like a marquee at an old movie theater. The squares spelled the phrase: "Only The Lonely." It was February, so I guess this was some cruel nod to the holiday that bisects it. Thus it was appropriate, I suppose, that this was the decor the night I cried in the box—tears streaming, mascara running, shoulders shaking, snot dripping—forced to face the back wall, hoping no one would notice. People in the lobby probably thought I was pretending, playing along with the props. But I was actually crying big, dumb, untidy tears. Not because I didn't have a boyfriend, but because I did, and he wasn't around for that stupid, stupid holiday.

Pretend I didn't tell you that.

I had feigned indifference, acted like I could care less about the stupid holiday. *What a dumb, commercialized load of crap*, I'm sure I'd said. Here's a tip: If your significant other ever says anything remotely similar to this, don't believe him or her. Maybe some people really do mean it, but I'd always err on the side of St. Valentine, just to be safe. Even my most black-hearted friends bleed mush when flowers arrive on their doorsteps. I know this because they will proudly post pictures of such gestures on Facebook or Instagram with the hash tag #lovehim or #bestboyfriendever.

It was our first Valentine's Day together, and with a craziness that only a twenty-something in a brand new relationship can possess, I thought this meant something. But of course, like a twenty-something in a brand new relationship, I didn't tell him this. I expected him to read my mind, to just *know*.

I don't know why I cared, really. I've never had a good relationship with the holiday, ever since Valentine's Day my freshman year in high school. I had my very first boyfriend and, because of that, it was my first Valentine's Day that mattered. School was cancelled because it was a snow day, so my boyfriend invited me over to his house. Before I had even taken off my coat, he handed me two pink carnations and a candle that looked like a mushroom. Then, before I could even say thank you, he dumped me.

The next day, I couldn't go to school, couldn't get out of bed. I learned why they call it heartache. Your actual heart— not the round-edged red one in the Hallmark window, but the one inside your chest with aortas and ventricles, that one— physically aches.

Pretend I didn't tell you that, either.

The boyfriend that I was crying about in the box recovered, slightly, when an orchid the size of an adolescent showed up outside my apartment. I read the card while standing outside, still in my pajamas. It told me not to worry, that we had a life-time of Valentine's Days to spend together.

Pretend I didn't—no, never mind. You can remember that one. His name is Peter.

Waitress

■

There are a few words or phrases in the "industry"—meaning "restaurant industry"—that make me cringe. "Industry" being one of them. Even more unpalatable is "Industry Night," a mixer typically held on a Monday, so employees from local establishments can get together and enjoy three-dollar shots. It also never sat well with me when a restaurant employee, who had just arrived at work at 5:00 pm, said, "Good morning!" Worse still was when they'd refer to their days off as the "weekend" when it was nowhere near a weekend. "Have a great weekend!" the bartender would shout over his shoulder when finishing a shift on Monday, knowing he wouldn't be back to work until Thursday.

Most cringe-inducing, however, was when the staff would refer to one another as "family." At the end of my first week at the restaurant, the manager hooked his arm around my shoulder and proclaimed, "Well, you're part of the family now." He rattled me into the crook of his arm, like something an uncle would do to a shy teenager. I thought he might give me a noogie. I lifted my head and looked around at these

Southern California strangers, three thousand miles away from my real home. Family? I was far from convinced.

This was not my first restaurant job. In college, I worked for a hot minute as a hostess at a Cuban-themed jerk-chicken-and-mojito joint. But that was for fun. To meet people. To have extra money for clothes and beer. The people I worked with were also students, just making some extra cash. They were like me. They were *normal*. At the restaurant in Los Angeles, several of the employees were well over forty. Some of them were career servers and had worked there for ten, fifteen, twenty years. These people were not like me. *They must have had rough lives,* I thought. *Something must have gone horribly wrong.* And the ones my age, well, they had to be actresses, or from the wrong side of the tracks, right? These people worked there because they had to. But wait, so did I.

The place I begrudgingly called "home" three to four days a week was Chaya, an upscale Asian-fusion restaurant in Venice. After twenty-five years, it was still consistently busy, a go-to spot on the Westside where agents took clients, businessmen schmoozed investors, and celebrities who lived in the neighborhood drank sake, safe from the paparazzi that preyed on the city's more interior restaurants. It was also a restaurant where Chelsea Handler had worked to support herself while doing stand-up, until (legend goes) she was eventually fired for chasing a customer into the parking lot when he failed to leave a tip. Another legend says that she was actually fired because she was always drunk. This I find more believable. I worked in the same section she had, the cocktail lounge, which attracted every walk of life: the Ladies Who Cosmo (even though the Cosmo fad was long gone), the yoga-mat-wielding green tea–drinkers, the surfers, the Venice hipsters, the young and successful, the couples with strollers, the repellent old men.

The old men were the worst. "Has anyone ever told you, you look like you ride horses?" one of them said, while cracking an imaginary whip in the air. He then let out a "Yee-haw!" and spanked his thigh. Another time, a man in sweatpants and a red bandana, fresh from Gold's Gym, asked, "Now on this entrée—could you ask the chef if I could get a female chicken?"

Huh?

Women asked the most ridiculous questions, too.

"Can I get you started with something to drink?" I asked a woman who took a seat in my section.

"Oh, there will be two of us," she said, panicked, when I only put down one cocktail napkin. I have decided there are two types of people in this world: people who are comfortable eating by themselves, and people who are decidedly not.

"I'm waiting on someone," she reiterated, terrified I might have thought for a second she was all by herself. A moment later, she asked, "Now this wine, the Cabernet Sauvignon, it's caffeine-free right?"

I looked up from my notepad. "Yes," I said. "All of our wine is caffeine-free."

If I learned anything from working at a restaurant, it's that, generally speaking, people are insane.

At the end of a shift during my first week, while separating ones from twenties—excited about this stack of cash but terrified that I had to calculate how much I was supposed to tip out—one of the servers saw me mashing the calculator's clear button like a chimpanzee. She asked if I needed some help. When we finished my checkout, she invited me to join some of the girls for a late-night meal down the street. "Sure," I said, because I was hungry, not because I was in the mood to make new friends. (I love friends but I don't like making them. It's just so much work. I hate the beginning of anything—a job, a class, the get-to-know-you games, caring what you look like, making a good impression. I wish I could just skip to already knowing each other, liking each other, and not caring what each other thinks.)

We sat in a large leather booth at Swingers, a '60s-style diner on Lincoln Boulevard in Santa Monica, all wearing our server uniforms: some of us in the all-black ensemble of the cocktail waitresses, others in the shirt-and-tie combo required for the dining room. I ordered a grilled cheese and tomato soup and barely said a word. Which was very strange for me. But I was in such a weird place. I had just broken up with a boyfriend and had just quit my real job. Now I was paying for a grilled cheese sandwich at one in the morning with a wad of ones pulled from an apron that was still tied around my waist. *What the hell is going on*, I thought. *I'm a waitress.*

■

Because I spent so much time at that place, you'd think I'd be rolling in money. The problem was, for my first year at the restaurant, I had to work at the sushi bar before I could move into the much more lucrative cocktail section. This meant I left each night with maybe sixty bucks. Heather and I lived together at this point; we'd graduated from sharing a bed-room to sharing a two-bedroom apartment. (Craving weather patterns and closed-toed shoes, Melissa and Rachel had both fled to foggier pastures in San Francisco.) During that period, Heather was my sugar mama on more occasions than I'd like to admit. She often hooked me with, "I'll buy you dinner if you clean the house." Said from her real office where she made real money. More months than not, I'd pay my rent part-check, part-cash-from-tips, part-IOU. At one point, my running tab with her flirted dangerously close to four digits.

On days when I worked at both *Flaunt* and Chaya, I'd leave the magazine in Hollywood at four o'clock and race west on the 10. I'd slam into a spot, change into my server uniform behind the tinted windows of my backseat, and barrel up the parking garage ramp, passing under a sign that said NOT A WALKWAY while stuffing my feet into my shoes. I'd zoom through the employee entrance, saying "Hola!" to the Hispanic cooks in the kitchen, "Konichiwa!" to the Japanese chefs at the sushi bar, and "Sorry" to the manager for being late.

By all accounts, I was one of the worst cocktail waitresses of all time. There are some pretty significant reasons I should have never been a server: I am clumsy, I am forgetful, and I am very bad at pretending to be in a good mood when I'm not. The best adjective to describe my serving skills was "clunky." I'd try to channel my inner geisha, their delicate hands gingerly pouring tea, their faces in a perfect, painted pout, all while wearing a beehive and little wooden blocks for shoes. I possessed none of that grace.

Coordination has never been my thing. I have always been terrible at sports with teams and/or balls, though I have played them all. One time, in third grade, my grandparents flew up to stay with me while my parents were out of town, and they came to my soccer game. The coach never put me in. Not once. Throughout the entire game, two other unskilled players and I were skipping along the sidelines, involved in our own intense competition of who could catch the most falling leaves. After the whistle blew, one of them realized she hadn't gotten to play, and she started crying. The coach, feeling sorry, said he'd start us all in the next game. This was doubly punishing for me. I had let down my grandparents, who had traveled so far, and now I had to *start* in the next game? I spent the whole next week praying the ball wouldn't come anywhere near me. When it did, I panicked and kicked it out of bounds. Soon after, thankfully, I was taken out of the game and able to continue leaf catching, an activity at which I was much more adept.

The coordination that evaded me on the field was missing from my server arsenal as well. I once spilled five beers on one person. I was carrying six different bottles for six different men—a little army of Stellas, Heinekens, and Amstels, all balancing perilously on my unsteady tray. I placed the Stella in front of the guy who ordered it (or one can hope), and then something went horribly wrong. I'm not sure how. Maybe I lost my balance. Maybe I hit the tray with my own hand. Maybe I had a seizure. But all five beer bottles dove off the tray—*BANG, BANG, BOOM, SHATTER, SPLASH*—right into this poor guy's lap. Fortunately, he was a good sport about the whole thing. "At least I told my wife I was going to the bar tonight," he said, sniffing his soaked shirt as I fumbled to fork over a stack of napkins.

My coworkers would often ask why I didn't work in the dining room. "You could make so much more money," they'd say. Honestly, the more casual ambiance of the cocktail lounge was treacherous enough. In the dining room, I would have probably lit someone's hair on fire.

The managers liked to joke that what I lacked in skill I made up for in charm, because rarely were my tips below twenty percent, and the five-beers-one-lap scenario was only one of many such debacles. Charm, maybe, if I was in a good mood. More like charm and humor—and honesty.

When customers asked how certain things tasted, I told them exactly what I thought. About the vanilla ginger gimlet, I'd reply, "It tastes like Pine-Sol, or air freshener. It tastes like something you're supposed to smell but not eat." About other items, say the New Zealand grass-fed lamb chop, I'd tell customers, "I have no idea. I've never had it." They'd look at me, confused, and after I'd give them the ol' "honest-to-goodness" shrug, they'd laugh and thank me. On many nights my tables would really stump me with, "What are the specials?" See, here's the thing. I worked in the cocktail lounge. Sure, customers could order off the dining room menu, but most people ordered from the bar menu, which I knew inside and out, if for no other reason than I selected my dinner from it nightly. When asked this very standard question, I'd reply,

"You know," pointing my pen at them, "that is a great question." I'd pause for effect. "That I do not know the answer to. But if you wait one minute, I'll race into the back and find out. You want to time me?"

A good cocktail waitress (I am using the antiquated word "waitress" because we were all girls), would have always known the specials and would have always let her tables know that they could also order off the much more expensive dining room menu, in addition to the relatively cheap bar food menu. But that was another area of my server brain that just didn't fire: I absolutely hated selling.

I have always lacked that inherent salesperson get-up-and-go. I never up-sold a thing. If a customer asked for water, I never even let them know that we also had six-dollar bottles of Pellegrino and Evian. I don't think I once asked a table if they'd like "coffee, tea, espresso, desserts?" The words echoed throughout the night from other servers, but the only time I'd suggest a table have dessert is if they were my friends and I wanted to eat some of it.

Not only did I lack salesmanship, but half the time, I'd talk people out of stuff. "Oh god, no, you don't want that," I'd say, about the fresh mint tea. "It tastes like hot toothpaste."

Behavioral studies say that servers can increase their tips by one, or a combination, of the following: touching a person lightly on the shoulder, writing "thank you" on the check, introducing themselves by name. I never did any of those things. My name alone was a disaster. "Lila-what?" it typically began. It never ended quickly. "How do you spell it?" "Where does that come from?" "Where are you from?" "What are you doing out here?"

When the managers started posting customers' Yelp reviews on the employee bulletin board in the back, I dreaded the name thing even more. From then on, if my tables asked my name and I thought my service hadn't been so hot, I'd say,

"Jennifer." If I was fairly confident it had been good, I'd say, "Lilibet. L-I-L-I-B-E-T."

•

After only a few months, my cheap black work pants acquired a giant hole in the crotch, similar to a pair of chaps, and could only be worn under an apron. I told myself I wasn't going to spend money on new ones because I was going to quit. I told myself this for almost five years.

What I didn't know that first night at the diner, staring out the window onto an empty Lincoln Boulevard, was that those girls, who so kindly invited me along and who I so quickly dismissed, would become my sisters. My best friends. The backbone of my new life in Los Angeles. I would quickly learn every horrible presumption I made about them—and everyone else at the restaurant, for that matter—was totally unfounded. Almost none of the girls were actresses, and the ones who were worked hard at it. Not to mention I myself would eventually become "one of those girls" who, from time to time, went on auditions. Two of the girls were in nursing school, and a couple others were getting master's degrees. Almost all of them were transplants like me, from the East Coast, the South, the Midwest. They were smart, interesting, independent women. And sure, one of those master's candidates was a former Hooters waitress, but who doesn't want a former Hooters waitress as a friend?

There were the sisters from Tennessee, Kathy and Victoria, who had moved to California to get away from Memphis, too nightmarish after both their parents had died. There was Madison, whose dad *arrested* O.J. Simpson—she can remember when the police helicopter landed in her cul-de-sac in Calabasas to scoop him up in his SWAT gear. I need no other reasons to be friends with someone. There was Jill from Oklahoma, one of those actresses who was really dedicated, and was also one of the funniest people I had ever met. One of the first nights we worked together, she told me a story about her pet dog eating her pet bird, and somehow she made it seem absolutely hilarious. I was sold. There was Noelle, one of the nursing students, who possessed the sort of calming presence and Gandhi-like advice that kept us all sane. In the chaos that is a restaurant job, Noelle was our human Xanax.

And then there was Junko (*Joon-koh*) who was from Japan. Junko was everyone's favorite employee. She was like a life-size My Little Pony. Her eyes were giant, almond-shaped, sparkly. Like a real pony, she was less than five feet tall. Though she had lived in LA for almost ten years and was completely fluent in English, she still sometimes had a tough time. The L's and the R's were, of course, a problem. There was an employee named Hillary that caused her all sorts of trouble. When Junko heard I was from Connecticut, she said, "Oh I love Connecticut! There are so many Bambis!" (She thought *Bambi* was the word for deer.) One time, she told us about a Japanese tradition in which everyone stays up all night on New Years Eve, and when the sun rises on the first day of the New Year, they all go outside and start crapping. (She meant clapping.) The language barrier sometimes caused problems while waiting tables as well. One night, Junko was waiting on an Italian man with a heavy accent. He ordered a *Chivas* (Regal, the Scotch whiskey), and twenty-five minutes later, Junko returned to the man's table with a *sea bass*.

The governess for all these girls was a gray-haired gay man named Jeffrey. He had worked at the restaurant for almost twenty years, and on his off days, he worked at a perfume shop. Nightly, he would bring us chocolates and perfumes and give us advice about men. He was like our very own *Golden Girl*.

Like Sophia, Jeffrey was never short on snark. I once asked if he and his husband ever went out to Rage or any of the other gay bars I was always passing on Santa Monica Boulevard.

"Oh, no, we don't go out dancing anymore," he said. "Now we just lie around and complain."

One night, Jeffrey answered the phone at the front desk because the hostesses couldn't get to it in time. A guest asked if she could get a reservation.

"MmmHmm," he said, never parting his lips.

"At eight o'clock?"

"MmmHmm."

"For two?"

"MmmHmm."

"Do you have valet parking?"

"MmmHmm."

"Thank you."

"MmmHmm." He never spoke a word. Later that night, the manager went up to him and said, "I just seated the 'MmmHmm' party."

We did these things to keep ourselves sane, especially during the recession. We leaned on each other during the recession because, as the economy went south, so did our business, and with that, our morale. A new memo from corporate appeared daily, one in English and one in Spanish—a *MEMORANDUM*, or the much more fun-sounding *MEMORANDO*.

"Employees are no longer allowed to consume espresso drinks during their shift, or beverages that require tea bags, milk, or chocolate sauce. If you would like to have an espresso-based drink during your shift, you may purchase it through the bartender at your forty percent employee discount."

A week later: "Due to tough financial times, the employee discount has now been reduced from forty percent to twenty-five percent." On that memo, an anonymous employee drew a graph with the "employee discount" running along the X axis and "morale" running along the Y, our collective mood dropping incrementally with the decreasing discount.

These memos went on for months:

"Employees are no longer allowed to use chopsticks, those are for guests only."

"Employees are no longer allowed to use the linen napkins in the bathroom. Paper towels will be provided for you in the back, which you can bring into the bathroom for your personal use."

At least, from a writer's perspective, each night at the restaurant was an adventure in idiocies uttered from the mouths of unsuspecting strangers. Where else could I hear things like, "So when I was in AA," from a man drinking a Kettle martini, up, with two olives, said with no sense of irony at all? Like my very own Easter egg hunt, I never knew when I'd wait on golden eggs like this particular mother-daughter pair: They both had heavy Japanese accents, and the mom barely spoke English, so her daughter ordered for them. She said, "I'll have a Diet Cock, and she'll have a regular Cock." About twenty minutes later the daughter signaled for me, motioned toward her mom, and said, "Could she have some more Cock please?" I had to walk away.

While situations like this were hilarious, others were more tedious. Waiting on large groups of women was what I feared most. Inevitably, one of them would wave me over in a panic, flailing her arms like she was stuck in a riptide, only to have me stand there for ten minutes while she and her friends discussed what to order, saying things like, "Now Meg, is it you or Karen who's not doing fried right now?"

"I'll give you ladies a few more minutes to decide and I'll come right back," I'd say.

"Oh, no no no, we're ready," one of them would demand.

Then they'd start ordering.

"No, Cind, that's too much tuna I think. Haven't you read about this mercury poisoning?"

"No I haven't," Cind would say.

"It's all over the news. Just yesterday I read something else in the—where was it? I can't remember. *The Times*. No, not *The Times*. It was the Huffington Post. No, that's not right either. It was—oh hell, Cindy, I can't remember."

All this while I'm still standing there, shifting my weight from side to side, scribbling furious little circles into my pad.

Once they finally got their food orders in, then they'd start specifying how they'd like their waters. Women were always particularly fussy about water. They wanted their water with no ice, or with ice and a lemon, or with ice but no lemon, or with light ice and two straws, or . . .

After sending me to various corners of the restaurant fetching a laundry list of items: a black napkin ("I just detest lint!"), a side of brown rice ("Much healthier than white!"), and more hot water for their green tea ("Good for cellulite!"), I'd finally get to drop the check. This, one would think, would be the best part of this whole operation. It was not. With large groups of men, one person would typically pay for the whole bill, or two would split it. With women, it got dissected down to the dime.

After much discussion and several minutes of iPhone calculating, seven credit cards would be tossed on the table. But the check would not be spilt evenly—no, no—because, as Karen emphatically noted, flicking a French-manicured nail against the check, she did *not* have a miso soup.

As irritating as these scenarios could be, they also provided endless amounts of entertainment for the employees. We'd place bets on how many ways a group of ladies would split the check—"I've got the over on five ways"—and we'd scatter like field mice when certain regulars arrived.

"Jill, you want 64?" I'd ask. "It's all yours."

"Are you sure?"

"Yeah, I'm exhausted."

Three minutes later, Jill would return from table 64, shaking her head and laughing. "I'm going to kill you." I had pawned the weird British guy off on her, the one who always sat at the same table and ordered a Kirin and a tuna "ta-ta."

One regular I avoided like he had SARS was a German man who always ordered half ice tea, half Diet Coke. Like that's a normal thing to order. To make matters worse, he was an incredibly bad tipper. I am not sure why Europeans pretend they don't know it's customary to tip twenty percent in American restaurants and continue to throw a pocketful of linty change on top of the bill. It's like, you know what? We're on to you. We know you know better. You're not fooling anyone, Hans.

In order to make this man his half ice tea/half Diet Cokes, I'd have to go all the way to the kitchen in the back to fill the glass with half ice tea, and then I'd have to go all the way to the bar in the front to have the bartender fill the rest of the glass with Diet Coke.

The bartender, Ted, was older than both my parents. He was a purist when it came to cocktails, believing drinks should be served neat—or, if one must taint the well, with water only. None of this club soda business. Ted was known to say, "What in the hell is this, a goddamned bachelorette party?" to a group of guys who ordered Kamikaze shots or mojitos. Invariably, when I placed the half glass of ice tea on the bar and asked him to add some Diet Coke, Ted would say, "Well what in the hell is already in there?"

"See that man at table 68, the one in the neon windbreaker? He wants a half ice tea/half Diet Coke."

"Well that is the craziest damned thing I've ever heard."

No matter how many times this happened, Ted was as flabbergasted as if it were the first. After thirty years behind a bar, he had the memory of a goldfish; every trip around the bowl was a brand-new adventure. But even in his cantankerous way, there was a certain level of charm to Ted. I liked the guy.

It wasn't just the cocktail waitresses I formed intense bonds with, but the entire staff. Mark the manager used to call me the sister he never had. Except he had a sister. During those years, I spent more time with those people than anyone else in my life. We leaned on each other to distract ourselves from the endless hours on our feet.

At the restaurant, we were not allowed to use our phones. We'd be written up if we got caught. We were supposed to leave them in our cars or in our lockers, but no one did. I didn't even know where my locker was. Everyone kept them in their aprons, or in the drawers where they kept their credit card slips. We'd all steal glances at various moments throughout the night, but not very often. I honestly think this is why our friendships were so strong. No one was ever tapping buttons or touch-screens while they talked. No one was compulsively checking texts mid-conversation. We were looking each other in the eyes, talking. Sure, we'd run off every now and again to check on a table, but we always came right back and finished our conversations.

For eight hours a night, four nights a week, we waited in the well while our drinks were made, stood shoulder-to-shoulder folding stacks of starchy napkins, shared meals on sore feet while standing in the back. These people knew every detail of my life, and I knew everything about theirs. "How's your grandfather doing?" they'd ask, when the rest of my friends didn't even know he was sick. These were the people who wondered where I was if they hadn't seen me for a few days. Who would call to make sure I was okay. They were the people I drove to the vet when their dog was sick, the ones who picked me up when my tire was flat. These were airport-ride people. We knew each other's moods immediately. We finished each other's sentences. We laughed so hard we cried. We cried so hard we laughed.

■

For my last shift at the restaurant, the classic rock station was playing all night—Lynyrd Skynard, The Band, Tom Petty, Pink Floyd. Everyone was complaining, but I was thrilled. At the end of most shifts, the cocktail servers would share a dessert. That night, I got to pick my favorite: chocolate croissant bread pudding. When it came out, it was covered in candles and, written in chocolate, it said, *Good Luck Lilibet, We Love You!*

"Imagine" came on the stereo, and I started to cry. I loved them too. As much as it pains me to use the term in this context, these people—every one of them—were my family. I used to think that if "The Big One" hit, I'd want it to happen while I was in there, with all of them.

Anatomy of a Haircut

I'd sometimes take pictures of myself in the box, using the Photobooth application on my laptop. This was before the advent of the "selfie," back when taking pictures of yourself was still something to be embarrassed about. I'd have to position my laptop so the pinhole camera was centered on me just right, and then I'd pretend I was looking at something else when I snapped the picture. Or, I'd pretend I was looking at an interesting website, or sometimes I'd pretend like I was *smiling* at an interesting website, as if that wasn't obvious. I don't know why I went to any lengths to pretend I wasn't taking a picture of myself, because as soon as my computer's camera flashed, the box was illuminated, and the gig was up.

In one of these pictures, I appeared to be sitting in a forest. That month, the box was painted like a very elementary Bob Ross creation: bushy evergreens, wispy white clouds, royal blue sky, emerald green grass. The photo is cropped just below my collarbone, and I looked naked. There were no straps, no sleeves, just skin. That night I had taken a real Box Girl fashion risk. No, I was not actually naked; I was wearing a strapless white body suit from American Apparel, which is basically a tube top with a crotch. I cannot remember what compelled me to wear a strapless white body suit that night, but I can remember that this was a time in my life when most everything I wore was from American Apparel.

In the photo, my lip gloss was a shade of "dusty rose," if something glossy could be described as dusty. It was obviously applied while sitting in the box, without a mirror, because it was askew, not fully covering my lower lip, but just the middle of it, like a geisha. This created the illusion that my mouth wasn't quite aligned. My eyes were lined in brown, and my eyebrows looked like two miniature ferrets crawling across my face.

Actually, I could only see one of my eyebrows because the other one was covered by a thick swoosh of asymmetrical bangs. Which brings me to The Haircut. My hair was feathered into an asymmetrical mullet and flipped out at the end like a '70s Florence Henderson, before she morphed into a bizarro Hillary Clinton. The haircut originated with a part that was *way* left, like comb-over left, then cascaded over the crest of my head, tapering out just below eye level, before snaking down the right side of my face in a loose S-shape, hugging the curves of my cheekbone. At lip level, it flipped out like Florence's, and the whole affair came to a halt just above my shoulders. This haircut was quantifiably ugly. It really was. But was it so ugly it was hot? I'm afraid, at the time, I was under that impression.

Gertrude Stein said, "Those traits of ours which most embarrass us when we are young, we later come to see as our charms." In my case, this thing I once believed so charming now embarrasses me.

The most amusing thing about this haircut was that I got paid to do it. One night at the restaurant, I was waiting on a stylist for a hair care company, and she needed some models for a hair show that Saturday. I had never heard of a hair show. She said it was a big convention at The Staples Center, where all the hair manufacturers showcase their products. She wanted my coworker Victoria to do it, too. We told her we'd think about it and let her know the following day. I had never cut my hair more than two inches at a time—I had always wanted to, I'd just always been too scared. Throughout the night, Victoria and I weighed the decision, discussing the pros and cons. We held our hair up behind our heads in the bathroom mirror to see what it would look like. And maybe we were exhausted, maybe we were "tasting" wines that night, but by the end of our shift, we had convinced ourselves that having our hair cut by a stranger for a hair show was a genuinely good idea.

Two days later, we went to the woman's "hair studio" in Marina del Rey. It was her house. She positioned us against a wall in her kitchen and took "before" pictures. That is when I started to get nervous. She offered us glasses of white wine, which we thought was weird but we eagerly accepted. Before I knew it, my hair was hitting the ground in eight-inch strands. I told Victoria to get the bottle of wine; I needed a refill. When she finished, my hair was so short in the back, I actually had a ducktail. The front was asymmetrical, not only in its extreme side part, but because one side was longer than the other. This was "a look," the stylist assured me. While looking at myself in the mirror I kept dipping my head to the side to make the sides of my haircut even.

The next day, we had to be at the Staples Center by 7:00 AM in black tops and black pants. I hadn't slept the night before because I was on a magazine deadline. I finished the piece around five in the morning and lay on my floor, facedown by the electric heater, too tired to sleep. I eventually peeled myself up, and when I walked into the bathroom to take a shower, my reflection startled me. There is something very unsettling about not sleeping and then suddenly remembering that the day before (or is it still the same day if you haven't slept?) you had all of your hair chopped off. There is something even more unsettling about not sleeping, realizing you let a stranger cut off all your hair, and then having to shake hands and smile next to a Jumbotron of your "before" picture. (Which, by the way, she told us not to smile for.)

■

Looking at the photo of me in the Bob Ross box installation, I can tell it was taken a couple of months after the hair show because the ducktail had grown into a sort of shaggy neck covering. In the picture, both of my eyes are darting skeptically, silently asking, "Why am I in woods with no clothes on?" I was trying to be ironic. Because everything was ironic back then; I was *filled* with snark. This was during my "hipster" phase, if we must use that word.

An NPR comedian once described hipster girls as taking someone who is probably smoking hot, then putting her in a floral dress from the Salvation Army that smells like moth balls, lacing her up in some beat-up barn boots that make her look like she should be trying out for *Newsies,* maybe adding a man's hat, and removing all of her makeup except for some ironically dark lipstick.

Who wanted long, beautiful, well-conditioned hair anyway? That was just too obvious. Way too mainstream. Instead, I'd cut my hair like a little Dutch boy and flip it just so as I swayed back and forth at The Echo, my arms crossed and my back hunched over, while sipping a Pabst Blue Ribbon and listening to a band you've never heard of.

This haircut said "I'm hip." This haircut said, "I get it." This haircut said, "Yeah, I know that band." This haircut said, "Obviously I am going to Coachella."

This haircut attracted a particular type of guy. They normally had mustaches, which they, too, thought were so ugly they were hot. Most of them lived east of Vermont Avenue, in Los Feliz or Silverlake or Echo Park, and it was during this time that I used to say I was moving over there. I would complain that the Westside was so Westside-y, with its Nordstrom and Starbucks and moms always in workout clothes. I wanted the thrift stores, the farmer's markets, the fair trade coffee shops.

Like the haircut, this phase didn't last. They never do. Now I can't imagine living all the way in Silverlake, so far from Venice and the rest of my life. Some days I don't even see the ocean, but I like to know it's there.

Entourage

■

From: Lilibet Snellings[7]

To: Undisclosed Recipients

Date: Wed Apr 25, 2007 at 2:26 pm

Subject: entourage

Mailed by: hotmail.com

I shot an episode of entourage on Monday. My role was 'bikini girl' it was hilarious. When the episode airs we all have to tivo it so we can re-watch my 25 seconds of fame over and over again. Holla!

Ignore the fact that at one point in my life (2007, age twenty-four) I thought it was acceptable to close an email with "Holla!" (Not even "Holler" but "Holla." Did I think I was Jay-Z? Gwen Stefani?) Let's take a moment to break this bad boy down. The first thing that needs to be noted: This email with the capitalized

---

7 This is the actual email.

day of the week but the un-capitalized TV show title was sent to multiple contacts. I mass emailed the word "Holla." Who it was sent to, it's hard to say, as this message was resurrected from the crypts of my Hotmail account. I can tell you that, at that very moment in time, I sincerely believed I was going to be on camera for at least twenty-five seconds, and possibly even become famous from such screen time.

Calling my role "bikini girl" is also misleading. I was an extra—who was, yes, in a bathing suit, but so were at least two hundred other extras. Did I think all of us were going to get credit for our roles on IMDB? Bikini Girl #1, Bikini Girl #65, Bikini Girl #194. I got this role through one of my former bosses at the agency. She IMed me and asked if I wanted to be an extra on *Entourage*. Though I did not yet have headshots, and had not yet been on my first commercial audition, as you can see based on my Holla-ing, I was more than enthusiastic about the idea.

The extras were told to meet in the Robinsons-May parking lot on Wilshire Boulevard at 7:00 AM. From there, we'd be bussed to the shoot location. We were also told to bring a couple of different bikinis, so a prop stylist could choose one for us. When my name was called, I entered the wardrobe trailer with my options in an American Apparel tote bag. She thumbed through my selection, finally settling on a pink and white polka-dotted number with some very small bottoms.

The busses dropped us off at the W Hotel in Westwood, where we'd be shooting by the pool. After de-bussing, I spotted my friend Maggie. While I knew Maggie was a sometimes-actress, I had no idea she'd be there. "If they ask for volunteers to get in the pool, we have to raise our hands," she said. "That way we'll get a 'wet bump.'" Maggie knew all the lingo. A "wet bump," she told me, was when the production company had to pay extras more money because they got wet. There was also a "smoking bump," for extras willing to smoke a cigarette.

One of the director's assistants came out and said he needed half the extras to take seats on the poolside lounge chairs, and the other half to be walkers passing by the pool. Because we knew there was no bump for walking, we dove for two chaise lounges. Next to them were fake cocktails. Mine was a gelatinous green gel that was supposed to look like an apple martini but looked more like a glassful of Aloe Vera. Adrian Grenier's character, Vince, and Kevin Connolly's character, Eric, would be sitting by the pool, talking to two British girls. The extras were instructed to talk and drink and hang out like we were enjoying a regular Monday afternoon at a hotel pool. Except we were not actually allowed to talk; we had to mimic talking without saying any words, which is not the most natural thing to do. While mouthing, "This is so fun. This is SO fun. THIS is so fun," over and over again, I found myself overdoing it with the hand gestures, feeling as if I needed to rely on them, in lieu of a voice, like a deaf person.

About thirty minutes into the poolside miming, the director asked if anyone was willing to get in the pool. Either these girls did not know about the "wet bump," or they just didn't want their spray tans to wash off, but Maggie and I were the only people who actually jumped off their lounge chairs. The director eventually wrangled a couple other girls and two guys, one of whom had halitosis and proceeded to follow me around the shallow end for the better part of the day. (Please imagine, for a moment, what an affront halitosis is when one is told to just "breathe" the words, not say them.)

Fortunately, I got some reprieve during a quick break for lunch, though I noticed there was a collective lack of enthusiasm for food when everyone was dressed in bikinis. After lunch, the director asked if anyone was willing to swim across the pool, underwater. I'd clearly inhaled too much chlorine because I shouted, "I'll do it!" as if he had asked for a volunteer to make out with Adrian Grenier. Perhaps I was under the impression there was such a thing as a "really wet bump." There is not. In addition to that, let me explain something about my swimming skills: I don't have any. I can string together enough aquatic aptitude not to die, but beyond that, there's not much to work with. If I swim one length of your standard twenty-five-meter pool, I am grabbing onto the wall at the end, gasping for breath, coughing up chlorinated water. People are often curious about this. "Doesn't endurance from running translate to swimming?" they'll ask. I can say with conviction, it does not. I can run six miles and look like I've only done a jumping jack or two, but if I swim a couple of laps, I'm not right for days.

To be clear, the director had said he needed a volunteer "to swim across the pool." While I now realize that could be taken in the plural, I took it to mean that he needed someone to get from one side to the other, once. It was a small pool, much smaller than the one at the gym that had made me see white. If I pushed hard enough off the wall, I figured, I'd basically already be at the other end. The director told me I was to swim across the pool, underwater, then emerge from the water, walking slowly up the steps. Then I was to stroll around the side of the pool, passing by Adrian Grenier and Kevin Connelly. Well, I thought, with that level of direction, and that much action for my character to take on, I had basically just been upgraded to a series regular. As I slow-walked around the pool in a bikini, I'd be the object of the two main characters' eyes. This would be my Phoebe Cates in *Fast Times At Ridgemont High* moment. My breakthrough. Lord only knows who would be banging down my door after such a performance.

I clung to the ledge in the deep end, ready for takeoff. When the director said, "Rolling," I was to push off the wall and begin my swim to stardom. I glided across the bottom of the pool, underwater, opening my eyes halfway through so I didn't slam into the stairs, then held onto the railing with the poise of a ballerina and sashayed up the steps. As I rounded the corner, I made sure to make some serious eye contact with Adrian Grenier. If the director didn't love me, then maybe he'd say something on my behalf: "What about that polka-dot bikini girl? We should find a recurring role for her."

When the director said, "Cut," I was certain I had done what it takes to win over not only the director and the stars, but the hearts and minds of America. I figured a prop stylist would be scurrying out at any minute with a terrycloth robe with my name monogrammed on the back and a cup of herbal tea, ready to escort me to a trailer they were no doubt redecorating for me at that very moment. I was snapped out of my day-dream when the director addressed me directly: "Swimmer!" he said. "Back in position." Oh. I had to do it again? Had I not absolutely nailed it on the first attempt?

I readied myself in the deep end, pushed off the wall, and did two frog-like strokes to get across the pool. Then I walked up the steps and around the pool. I would perform this combi-nation of maneuvers at least twenty-five times.

After only a few passes, my very short haircut was matted to the sides of my head like a rugby helmet. After several more takes, my sinuses were filled with snot, my fingers were past the point of prune, and the skin on my hands was transparent, like rice paper. My eyes were bloodshot and watering like an addict on the fourth day of a meth bender in the Appalachia. I was dizzy. Exhausted. Freezing. I no longer cared about the "wet bump." I would have taken a "dry cut" to get me back on that chaise. I would have taken a "double dry cut" to get me into my bed. That day, I learned a valuable lesson in show business: They never do one take. They never do twelve takes. They do one million and fifty-five takes. And then, just before nightfall, when you've lost all hope, when you've resigned yourself to the fact that you will die on the set of *Entourage*, the director says, casually, "That's a wrap."

As the bus barreled back to the Robinsons-May shopping center, I was comforted by one fact: I was going to be all over the camera. I might have been waterlogged, and my lips might have been blue, but my fifteen minutes of fame were due.

I immediately told everyone I knew. I told my coworkers at the restaurant and the magazine. I called my parents. I sent a blast email with the word "Holla" tacked at the end. People told other people, and every time someone told someone else, my role became significantly more substantial. "Bikini Girl," which was already a stretch, morphed into "Guest Star," which morphed into "Recurring Series Regular," which morphed into "Dating Adrian Grenier in real life." And who was I to correct anyone?

Three months later, the episode aired. There were watch parties.

Okay, there were not watch parties, but a lot of people watched. I watched from my apartment, by myself, my stomach twisted into knots with anticipation.

Exactly five minutes and eighteen seconds into the episode there was a very, very, *very* overhead shot of the W Hotel pool. It looked like it was taken from outer space. In the center of that pool was something that looked like a tadpole, or a sea monkey. From exactly 5:18 to 5:20, that tadpole swam, for two underwater strokes, across the pool. Then the camera cut to a close-up of that tadpole emerging from the pool: blonde, tan, and toned . . . with a camouflaged bikini and a large lower-back tattoo. I watched in disbelief. I rewound on my TiVo. Every time I watched her taught, tattooed body get out of the pool, it was harder than the last. Who was this imposter? Was this my body-double? What was wrong with my un-tattooed body? While I was apparently fine to use for the camera angle that was shot from a satellite, for the close-up, I didn't make the cut. I imagined the editors' conversation:

"Well, the swimmer girl looks a little banged up," one would say.

"Yeah, she looks like she's sort of struggling to get out of the pool," the other would add.

"Plus, that rose bush back tattoo is *hot*."

I continued to watch anyway, hoping they'd flash back to the pool scene, thinking maybe there was still a chance. About a quarter of the way through the episode, they cut back to the W Hotel pool. The camera closed in on Adrian Grenier and the brunette British girl. At eight minutes, twenty-five seconds, there I was again: side-profile, a pixilated smudge of myself in the background wedged between both their heads. The camera cut to Kevin Connolly and the blonde British girl for a moment, and then slowly made its way back left. As it panned across the pool, I could see the guy with the halitosis wading by the stairs. The camera then stopped for a while on Adrian Grenier and the brunette. Maggie was visible for most of the scene, even in the background, while I was entirely blocked by the British girl's head. I could see Maggie pretend-talking to me and, peeking out from behind the large head in the foreground, I could see my right hand dramatically gesturing back.

Signs That You Have Made It

You can shave your legs without hitting your head
   against the wall of the shower.

You can't vacuum your entire home without unplugging
   the vacuum.

Your bed doesn't have to be crammed in the corner of the
   room.

Your bed is not the "double" your parents bought for your
   sophomore year in college.

You have a dishwasher.

You have a washing machine.

Your refrigerator makes its own ice.

Your refrigerator has food in it.

You don't have to work in the box.

Signs That You Have Not Made It

■

Your credit card company asks if you've considered a new line of work.

Hooters vs. The Box

■

When my girlfriend at the restaurant told me she used to work at Hooters, I eyed her tiny, ninety-five-pound frame and couldn't help but notice she was lacking a key ingredient for the job.

"I know," she said. "I don't have big hooters." She seemed more than happy to go on. "The girls who didn't have big boobs or implants wore two padded bras on top of each other, and we put our Hooters T-shirts over that. It worked really well."

Hold the mail. What? I couldn't believe it. It felt like learning Dolly Parton stuffed with shoulder pads.

My friend's stories from Hooters made me appreciate the restaurant where I worked. At Hooters, she said, the servers were encouraged to egg the men on. That was the point. Eat a basket of wings, drink a pitcher of beer, look at a roomful of hooters (or padded bras under T-shirts, *idiots*) and flirt with your waitress. She said Hooters girls were required to sit at each table for at least a few minutes—bat their pretty little eyes, bait the men. "That was a requirement. If we were folding napkins or talking to each other, the manager would come over and say, 'Go sit down with your customers.'"

Hooters girls also had to leave a cocktail napkin on each table with their name written on it and "some sort of flair" (she was a smiley-face girl). On slow days, she said, whoever had the most napkins with their names on them could go home early. "It was funny; the guys thought you were giving them your name to flirt with them, but really you just wanted to be sent home early." Another requirement: They had to ask each table if they wanted fries, no matter what. "That's why people think Hooters girls are dumb," she said, laughing. "Two guys would go in and order cheesecake and we'd have to ask them if they wanted fries with that."

Every time a Hooters girl typed an order into the computer terminal, they had to print out the ticket, stand on a stool, and sling the ticket into the kitchen while yelling, "Hooters girls!" The rest of the Hooters girls would then have to stop what they were doing and say, in unison, "Oh, yeah!" There was a large Hooters Girls manual that outlined all of this. I found these details endlessly fascinating. My favorite part: In the back, there was a vending machine for the tights and socks they were required to wear. "Like a snack machine," she said, "Except it was full of nylons and '80s scrunch socks."

"Why the thick, shiny figure skater tights?" I asked.

"They suck everything in. Plus it makes you feel less naked. The shorts are so tiny."

My friend said she'd immediately tell all her tables she was in college, to distinguish herself from the other girls. "Apparently if you get a boob job while working at Hooters, you can write it off as part of your job, so a lot of girls were just working there for that." Others, she said, wanted to be Playboy Bunnies. "The Playboy people were in there recruiting a lot."

A Hooters girl's primary job, she said, was to look good. If you came to work and your hair wasn't down or your makeup didn't look good, you could be sent home. Hooters girls were also more than allowed to go out with the customers. "Guys would pull up in limos to pick them up," she said. "But you couldn't be seen leaving in your Hooters outfit, so everyone zipped Juicy velour sweat suits over their uniforms and left wearing that."

I would rather shoot myself. And I'm not talking about the Juicy Couture sweat suits. I can think of nothing worse than being required to lead on a stranger I have absolutely no interest in, especially after racing back and forth to fetch another couple rocks for his Scotch, *doll*; just a little more wasabi, *darlin'*; another napkin, mine fell on the floor, *sweetie*.

At the restaurant, some of the cocktail girls could work it. I could not. I couldn't even up-sell a dessert, let alone up-sell myself. I'd see some of the girls getting phone numbers from men who had said, "So, what else do you do? An actress, wow, what do you know? I'm a producer, I bet I could help you out." I'm sure plenty of these men were legitimately in the business, but I was always skeptical. I couldn't bring myself to be the damsel looking to be saved by someone who may or may not have been a producer—or a sex offender. It made my skin crawl. Another waitress friend of ours, Jill, couldn't do it either, and she was a real actress. When customers would ask what else she did, she'd say, dead seriously, "Nothing." Being a young girl in LA and *only* a waitress made people very uncomfortable. They'd smooth their napkins in their laps nervously. "Yep," she'd say, gazing gaily at her surroundings. "This is it!"

But why, I wondered, was I okay with wearing about as many inches of material as a Hooters girl when I was inside the box? At least they are bringing stuff to eat. I don't even come with buffalo wings. I am providing absolutely no service other than being something to look at.

I think the answer lies in the two-inch thick glass. In the box, I don't have to engage. I know a wall of glass separates me from them. I am protected in there. I don't have to interact, egg them on, flirt. I don't have to offer my name with a heart over the *i*. No one knows my name. I'm seen, I'm noticed, but I'm also left alone.

I Was A Box Bunny

■

In 1963, for her famous piece of undercover reporting, "I Was A Playboy Bunny," Gloria Steinem became a bunny herself, serving cocktails at The Playboy Club on East Fifty-ninth Street in Manhattan. She gave herself a new name (Marie Catherine Ochs) and a new age (four years younger than her real age, as she was beyond the bunny age limit). But, as she noted in the essay, she and Marie shared the same address, phone number, and most importantly, measurements and face. She could only mask so much.

Steinem embarked on this reporting assignment with a journal and an ad that read: "Attractive young girls can now earn $200-$300 a week at the fabulous New York Playboy Club, enjoy the glamorous and exciting aura of show business, and have the opportunity to travel to other Playboy Clubs throughout the world. Whether serving drinks, snapping pictures, or greeting guests at the door, the Playboy Club is the stage—the Bunnies are the stars." The ad went on to say: "If you are pretty and personable, between twenty-one and twenty-four, married or single, you probably qualify. No experience necessary."

During her Bunny interview, Steinem was told, "Sit over there, fill out this form, and take off your coat." The application was short: address, phone number, measurements, age, last three employers. The "Bunny Mother," a madame of sorts named Sheralee, took several Polaroids and looked over her application. Steinem tried to give the Bunny Mother a page she had fabricated about Marie's personal history, but the Bunny Mother resisted. "For the record," she said. "We don't like our girls to have any background. We just want you to fit the Bunny image."

Before Steinem knew it, she was being outfitted in her Bunny uniform, and the wardrobe mistress was stuffing an entire plastic dry-cleaning bag down the top of her bust. (Other items the Bunnies used for stuffing included Kleenex, cotton balls, cut-up bunny tails, foam rubber, lamb's wool, Kotex pads, silk scarves, and gym socks.) "Just about everyone stuffs," the wardrobe mistress told her. "And you keep your tips in there. The 'vault' they call it."

Like being a Box Girl, being a Bunny came with its own specific set of rules. The Bunnies could get demerits for a long list of things: wearing heels that were less than three inches, having runs in their pantyhose, wearing crooked or unmatched bunny ears, keeping an untidy bunny tail, and having underwear that shows. (Unlike Box Girls, Bunnies were probably encouraged *not* to wear underwear.) Messy hair, bad nails, or bad makeup cost them five demerits, while chewing gum or eating on the clock was ten. They were also required to react appropriately to the entertainers. If a comic was performing, then they had better laugh. For that matter, they were required to appear "gay and cheerful" at all times ("Think about something happy or funny," they were told).

Steinem received a copy of the Playboy Club Bunny Manual—
The Bunny Bible, as the Bunnies called it. The Bunny Bible suggested the following techniques for stimulating sales: "The key
to selling more drinks is customer contact . . . they will respond
particularly to your efforts to be friendly . . . You should make
it seem that their opinions are very important . . ."

Steinem also learned, "If Bunnies are meeting boyfriends or
husbands after work, they must do it at least two blocks from
the club." Playboy Club clientele were never to know the Bunnies had lives—or heaven forbid, husbands—outside the club.

The Bunny Bible also told the Bunnies they must "eye-contact" each of their guests immediately upon approaching their
table. I don't think I've ever heard the phrase "eye contact"
used as a verb, but the suggestiveness it takes on when re-
packaged as such makes me blush. To "eye-contact" someone
seems a lot more X-rated than simply "making eye contact"
with someone.

But, The Bunny Bible went on to firmly explain, the Bunnies were not allowed to give out their phone numbers or go
on dates with the customers. Nor were they allowed to give
out their last names. The Bunny Bible used the following to
illustrate this point: "Men are very excited about being in the
company of Elizabeth Taylor. But they know they can't paw
or proposition her. The moment they felt they could become
familiar with her, she would not have the aura of glamour that
now surrounds her."

Later, during the "Bunny Father Lecture"—a narrated slide-
show with jazz in the background—Steinem learned that, if
customers tried to "get familiar," the Bunnies were supposed to
politely reply, "Sir, you are not allowed to touch the Bunnies."
As Steinem points out, there is a problem here, a disconnect.
While the women were required to "eye-contact" and pamper
their customers, they were also obligated to reject them. As

soon as they seemed available, the Bunnies were apparently no longer desired.

This air of inapproachability has long been considered attractive. In the mid-nineteenth century, Edouard Manet caused an uproar when his painting "Olympia" was presented at the 1865 Paris Salon. What was so scandalous about this painting was not that the woman was completely naked—nudes had been painted for years—but that she was making direct eye contact with the viewer. I suppose you could say she was "eye-contacting" the viewer. Such forwardness was considered lewd, vulgar, and immoral. She should have been more demure, lying there with no clothes on.

The Standard, too, wants the Box Girls to be elusive and thus alluring, but not seductive in a comely "eye-contacting" sort of way. We are supposed to seem inaccessible, just ever-so-slightly out of the ogler's reach. In addition to no "eye-contacting," one Box Girl rule requires "light, natural makeup." They want us to be intriguing, but not in the lingerie, platform heels, and thick eyeliner tradition; rather, in the vein of girl-next-door-just-reading-on-her-floor. Even the uniforms, though there isn't much to them—all white, cotton—imply some sort of purity. It's wholesomeness, with a wink.

■

I wonder what Steinem would think of the box, if she would see it as something that is degrading to women. (Why do we *all* have to be women?) As a humanist, as well as a feminist, she might say, "Put men in there, too! Make it a true peek into human nature." I wonder what men would be required to wear.

I also wonder if Steinem would notice the obvious (though I don't think intentional) metaphor: a woman locked below a glass ceiling.

Interview

∎

"They're looking for a new blonde," was the way my friend Clare put it to me. A new blonde Box Girl at The Standard, she explained. Clare and I had worked together at *Flaunt,* and before that, she was a Box Girl.

She said I had to go in for an interview.

"An interview?" I asked. "What are they going to ask me? How skilled I am at sitting?"

She told me to meet the hotel's art director in the lobby at one o'clock.

While I waited, I looked at the empty box and tried to imagine myself inside it. I tilted my head to the side, squinted, tipped it to the other side. It was hard to imagine, but I was intrigued.

Before interviews, I am nervous. I normally prepare. But for this one, I didn't know what to prepare for. What could she possibly throw at me? The extent of my preparation was blow-drying my hair and fishing through my closet for something slimming and hip, something I thought a Box Girl would wear when she's out of the box.

The art director sat across from me on another couch. We talked for a few minutes about traffic, the weather, nothing. It wasn't really an interview at all; she spoke to me as if I already had the job and was just explaining it to me. The hours, parking, that sort of thing. I'm sure she just wanted to see what I looked like and make sure I wasn't totally insane. Toward the end of our chat, she ran through the rules, stressing, "Please wear light, natural makeup," and emphasizing "Absolutely no eye contact" twice. She asked if I had any questions. I looked at the box, shook my head, and said, "I mean, how hard could it be?"

The Zoo

■

A guy in a plaid flannel shirt is waving his arms overhead, trying to get my attention. He must not know I'm not allowed to look at him. And that must, I imagine, make this whole charade even more intriguing. If you say, "Here, kitty, kitty," and hold out your hand long enough, the animal at the zoo will at least give you a glance. She may even come over and growl, do something impressive. But I am contractually obligated to ignore you.

It's a bit peculiar to think that, if I have children someday, I will have to tell them about this job. "Oh, like the zoo!" I can hear them saying.

"Yes," I will be obliged to say. "Like the zoo."

But they'll already know all of this. They'll be able to mine the Internet for all sorts of former versions of their mom. As a child, I used to love looking through my parents' high school yearbooks. So involved in school activities, sports, and student government, my mom was on practically every page, smiling in her saddle shoes and Eton skirts. (As my Uncle George likes to say, she would have joined the "Tiddlywinks Club" if there were such a thing.) In my dad's yearbook, he was voted a "Snow Man," which he explained in the following way: "This was common slang in the sixties. A snowman was so 'cool' that he could produce 'snow' just by being himself. Girls in his vicinity were subject to being 'snowed,' a phenomenon that was often totally out of their control but generally not life-threatening. However, some young ladies who got thoroughly snowed often thought their life was over when the snowman did not embrace their infatuation." This, of course, is just one man's humble approximation of the phrase.

Sometimes, as a child, I'd find old photos in the backs of drawers or the bottoms of file cabinets. I kept one of my parents throwing a Frisbee in a park somewhere. My mom's hair was cut into a shaggy brown bob and she was wearing a short red romper. My dad, who I have never known without gray hair, had thick, golden-brown hair, styled into *muttonchops*. But the muttonchops were actually the least shocking part of the picture for me. What I really couldn't get over were his *cut-offs*. I have never in my life seen my dad out in public in anything other than pleated khaki pants. I have never seen him wear a single pair of jeans, let alone ones he took a pair of kitchen scissors to.

Other times I'd uncover a whole shoebox full of old photographs—the rounded-edge matte ones from the '70s and '80s—of my parents on a ski trip with friends, or at the beach. I loved seeing these versions of their former selves. While sometimes in the pictures it was pretty apparent that they were hammered drunk, that was about as scandalous as they got. Because, I'm sure, if there was photographic evidence of anything more illicit, those pictures would have been thrown away, or hidden in a shoebox that was harder for a child to find.

Back then, they had that luxury. They were keepers of a carefully curated photographic history. It was a much more civilized assortment. With the Internet, no matter how much erasing or unlinking I do between now and whenever I'd have a child old enough to dig around online, it will never be enough. The illustrated history of my generation is uncontainable. It is unbridled, unregulated, relentless.

Sometimes I Play Pretend

■

My first husband's name was Todd. He showed up in a T-shirt and jeans, which I thought was a touch underdressed, but he was polite and seemed like an all right husband all the same. Our child's name was Elsie. She was six years old and told me she had a zoo in her backyard. When I asked what kind of animals, she didn't have any specifics. Todd and I went through a lot together—a proposal, a pregnancy, and six-plus years of marriage—all in the fifteen minutes it took to audition for a Nationwide Insurance commercial.

The next time you are enjoying a relaxing stretch of TV, comfortably molded into your couch, take a moment to appreciate the hundreds of people who have made asses of themselves in the hopes of being in that commercial you're trying to skip.

At an audition for an "active lifestyle dating service" commercial, I recited the lines, "With my busy schedule, it's just so hard to meet people. I wish I could find someone who shares my passion for running and the outdoors"—while jogging in place. For a Cox High Speed Internet audition, I had various household items thrown at my head—an oven mitt, a ruler, a handful of markers—while an industrial-sized fan blew my hair. For a Capri Sun audition, I stood on the sideline of a make-believe field and cheered on my make-believe son, who was apparently playing soccer with other make-believe children. For a Bear Naked granola audition, I rode on the back of a German model named Rolfe while pretending we were on a hike. (Because don't you always hike with your boyfriend piggy-back style?) And I feigned true love at a Match.com audition. Yes, I hate to be the one to tell you, but the people on the commercials did not actually meet on Match.com. They met in the lobby of a casting facility on Beverly Boulevard in West Hollywood.

For some commercials, casting directors send blast notices to all of the actors who are signed up for a service called LA Casting. If an actor feels he fits the specs, he can submit himself for the project. These casting notices were a relentless assault on my inbox, a new one arriving every two to three minutes: SAG Nike Commercial, Monster Energy Drink Spec Commercial, Non-Union Target Commercial, Rush Call for Hyundai (Can anyone get to Studio City by 4:30?). I finally had to switch my LA Casting account to an old Hotmail email because these notices were draining my Blackberry's battery.

In the breakdowns, casting directors would describe the premise of the commercial and what type of actors they were looking for. I noticed they loved the word "aspirational" and always seemed to be seeking "aspirational-looking" people to cast in their commercials. How you can determine whether or not someone is "aspirational" from a headshot, I do not know. Were these actors gazing contemplatively at one corner of the headshot, like the man on the cover of *The Fountainhead?* Was one hand perched under their chin à la *Thinking Man?* I guess they just had that sparkle in their eyes.

Because I had worked on the agency end of things, I knew all the euphemisms. If the description said "Urban," it meant "black" and "sort of gangster." (See: Ludacris in *Crash*.) "Ethnically Ambiguous" was another one they tossed around frequently. Commercial casting directors loved ethnically ambiguous actors because they appealed to multiple markets. If they couldn't quite put their finger on what you were, all the better. I also knew that if I saw a casting notice for a "Dianetics Industrial," it was a commercial for the Church of Scientology.

Casting directors' wardrobe descriptions were equally entertaining. The oxymoron "Upscale Casual" was a favorite, along with the backhanded compliments: "attractive, yet approachable," or "attractive, but not a model."

"You're perfect," I could imagine a casting director saying to a young actress. "You're good-looking but not *that* good-looking."

I have seen the wardrobe description "Dog Park Cute" as well as "Carnival Date Casual," and I have also seen the request, "Seeking Pamela Anderson/Maxim types, but no one with a history of porn." For liquor and beer commercials, actors had to be "Legally Over 25 – WILL I.D. AT AUDITION." I almost submitted myself for a Heineken commercial once, before I read the full description of my role: "Has the ability to remain underwater for prolonged periods of time while wearing a mermaid tail."

In addition to commercials, I'd also receive casting notices for live events. This one was for an unnamed boot company: "We are looking for someone to wear a short dress or skirt or other appropriate outfit to highlight the boots. Duties include walking the show floor with an energized enthusiastic attitude to generate interest and excitement for the boots. MUST BE A SIZE 6 to 7. If you are a 5.5 or a 7.5 DO NOT SUMBIT!!!!"

I did not submit. My feet were too big. Plus, I wasn't sure I could generate the kind of excitement for the boots they were looking for.

I clicked on a male hand modeling notice once, out of morbid curiosity. I had to wonder if the guys who submitted themselves for this role had some serious complexes: "Adult hand model with child-sized hands. Hands should look like that of a 5- to 7-year-old boy."

I once submitted myself for a Joe's Crab Shack "Female Lunch Patron" audition and got called in. I was instructed to dress "nice casual," like I was "out to lunch with some friends." As soon as I got to the audition, it occurred to me that the other girls went out to lunch at different places than I did. Most of them were in four-inch heels. Who eats at a chain seafood restaurant in four-inch heels? I was in a pair of gold flats and a navy-and-white-nautical striped dress. If my outfit didn't say "casual lunch at a maritime-themed res-taurant," I don't know what did. For the audition, there were Fritos scattered on a table, which we had to pretend were crabs and eat with enthusiasm. We then had to pretend we were getting attacked by a very aggressive seagull. Unfortunately, my seafaring attire didn't compensate for the fact that I have absolutely no acting skills. I did not book the job.

The fact that I rarely booked any commercials didn't deter me from submitting myself anyway and Google-mapping my way across Los Angeles to go to the auditions. Because, if the casting notices were amusing, then the waiting rooms at these casting facilities were an absolute bonanza.

On the morning of my Nationwide audition, instead of commuting from my bed to my desk to play the role of "Writer" in the wardrobe of "Pajama Pants, T-shirt, and Slip-pers," I took a detour to the bathroom to take a shower, put on makeup, and blow-dry my hair. The assistant at the agency called me with the specifics the night before. Role: wife. Age Range: 25-35. Description: attractive yet approachable, not too model-y. Wardrobe: Upscale Casual.

It was hot that day, and the air conditioning was broken in my car. By broken I mean it had never actually worked. This left me with two unappealing options: 1) roll down all the windows to stay cool, which would whip my hair into a chaotic nest, or 2) keep the windows up and keep the hair in place, then arrive at the audition looking like I'd just left the steam room. When I left my apartment, freshly showered and deodorized, my hair slightly spritzed into its on-camera position, I looked like someone who could at least fake it as an actor, someone presentable enough to be in an insurance company commercial. But by the time I arrived at the audition I looked like exactly what I was: someone who didn't have health insurance.

Inside the casting facility, a giant flat screen read: "Quaker Oats: Room 1. Alltel: Room 2. Budweiser: Room 3. Nation-wide: Room 4." I took a seat outside room four and filled out my Size Card: name, agency, height, weight, bust, hips, waist, inseam, glove size, hat size. The last two—glove and hat size—I never knew and sometimes just wrote "regular" or "proportional."

I pulled out my book and pretended to read. At the far end of the waiting room were the Alltel guys—all in their mid-thirties, all dressed in suits, all with brown hair, all holding the same piece of paper. Some sat and read silently while others paced, pantomiming their lines. They became increasingly distracted, I noticed, as the room began to bustle with busty blondes arriving for their Budweiser auditions. I swear some guys only go to castings to pick up girls. And if they don't, they should. It's like a buffet. Everyone is skinny and pretty and be-tween the ages of twenty and thirty, and there are fifty or sixty of them in one waiting room, all in nearly identical outfits.

The Budweiser candidate to my right—platinum blonde hair, jeans, heels, low-cut top—seemed to be having some sort of dispute with a salon receptionist. "Well then can you *at least* squeeze me in for a pedicure?" she said, into her phone. The Budweiser candidate to my left—golden blonde hair, jeans, heels, low-cut top—recognized another girl—dirty blonde hair, jeans, heels, low-cut top—and greeted her with, "Heyyyyyyyyy. How are youuuuuuu?" The words dragged out like a wind-up doll that needed to be wound. The dirty blonde replied, "Oh my god I left my cell phone at home and I am like *totally* freaking out." The golden blonde responded, "Oh my god, that suuuuuuucks."

As I eyed these girls' perfectly curled and coifed locks, I tore my fingers through my hair, attempting to untangle its nautical-sized knots. I adjusted the collar on my shirt. I was wearing a blouse and slacks—two words I rarely use and two clothing items I rarely choose—but I was going for the conservative and responsible look. The insurance commercial look.

A few minutes later, the casting director emerged to inform me I would be auditioning twice since they had, at the moment, a shortage of women for the role of "wife" and a surplus of "husbands" and "children." He then explained that the Nationwide commercial would show three major snapshots of my life: the marriage proposal, the pregnancy, and then, cut to five years later, a portrait of my new little family.

Husband Todd entered, and we exchanged awkward hellos. For the first shot, we were told to sit on the couch and pretend we were watching TV, but we were really watching another chair across the room. Husband Todd was then instructed to—ever so casually—put his arm around me and dangle an imaginary engagement ring on an imaginary string, so it would lightly graze my right shoulder. I was told to notice this imaginary ring and gasp and smile and scream and look at this complete stranger, saying with orgasmic enthusiasm,

"Yes! Yes I will marry you!" And then we were to embrace in a jubilant hug.

For the next shot, I was told to stand in our pretend-living room, holding papers from the doctor's office that apparently informed me I was pregnant, while rubbing my belly and smiling into the distance. Husband Todd would then walk in, as if getting home from work, and see me smiling gleefully and rubbing my belly and *just know,* exclaiming, "Yeah?! Really, hon?! That's great! This is so great!" The casting director chimed in, "This is something you have both been hoping for, for a long time. Be sure to look as excited as your wife, husband."

For the final shot, the child actor joined us. Child actors always sort of scare me. So much bravado at such a young age. It's as if, at any moment, they might bust out a tap dance rendition of *Fiddler on the Roof.* It's unnerving. At any rate, Todd was told to pick up Elsie, and I was told to stand next to them, my arms around both, and smile like we were taking a family portrait at the softer side of Sears.

Todd and Elsie left and in came my next husband and child, Wes and Haley. Now, if there is anything more awkward than pretending to get married and have a baby with a complete stranger, it's pretending to get married and have a baby with someone you know.

"Lilibet? Is that you?" Wes was very confused. He was represented by the agency I used to work for, the agency that now represented me.

"Yes, it's me, hi!" I said.

"Oh my god, what are you doing here?" he said, leaning in for a one-armed hug. "I thought you were working at a magazine or something? Are you an actor now?"

"Yes, no. No I'm not an actor but yes I go on auditions sometimes," I said, rocking nervously in my sensible high heels. "I really have no idea what I'm doing," which I'm sure was super reassuring for him, considering he was going to be auditioning opposite me. Auditioning with someone who has no idea how to act is sort of like trying to play tennis with someone who has no idea how to play. You hit the ball to them, and they just stare at you blankly.

Wes was not the first former client I ran into while on an audition. I had several similarly awkward interactions. With the models, it was always, "You look so much thinner!"

"Well it's a lot easier to stay trim now that you're not sending me muffin baskets daily," I always wanted to say.

Like my first husband, Wes also interpreted "upscale casual" to just mean "casual." I was the only dope in the room dressed like someone whose day would be made upon hearing that there's cake in the conference room. Wes was clad in your standard East LA actor uniform: a partially un-tucked flannel shirt, the sleeves unevenly rolled, the collar not popped but not totally flat either—a calculated disarray, a level of disheveled-ness that can only be achieved with the finest attention to detail.

Our child was five and three-quarters and was missing her two front teeth. She told me she got twenty dollars per tooth. My mouth dropped open like a codfish. This may have seemed like an indication of astonishment, but really, it was jealousy.

Wes and I went through the same motions—the proposal, the pregnancy news, the glamour shots at Sears—in five or six minutes. My life's most momentous occasions were cranked out twice and packaged up tight, all for the sake of selling insurance. I always imagined I would someday get married, get pregnant, and have a child, or maybe even a few. I just never imagined all of this would happen with two different men, and within ten minutes, in a windowless room with coffee-stained carpet.

Walking out of the casting facility, I un-tucked my blouse and pulled my hair into a knot with the elastic I had accidentally left on my wrist during the audition. I took down my convertible's top—manually, of course—and kicked off my kitten heels, cracking my toes against the floorboard. The car's antenna was broken, so all that would come through on the radio was Mexican ranchero music. I reached into the backseat and grabbed the Case Logic that had followed me across the country years before. As I headed west on the 10, back toward the beach, and back toward my home, my BMW rattled along in the far-right-hand lane, the CD skipping with every bump in the road.

A Million Little Pieces (of Paper)

◼

I have this impulse to put things on paper—bits of dialogue I overhear, observations, anecdotes, funny old-fashioned sayings my Southern relatives slur after too many Scotch and sodas[8], lists of books I should have read by now, lists of films I should have seen by now, lists of words I should use but never do. All these things are scribbled on tiny pieces of paper. Hundreds of them. They're written on pulled-out pieces of notebook paper with the perforated edges still attached, on Post-it notes, corkboard coasters, coffee shop pastry bags, the corners of flight itineraries, the backs of bookmarks, the blank pages torn from the ends of books. I write these notes while I'm waiting in line at the grocery store, while I'm waiting for my hair to get highlighted, while I'm driving my car.

In Santa Monica one day, while getting honked at for holding up traffic, I scribbled on a carwash receipt: "Why does

---

8 Two of my favorites: "Don't worry about the horse going blind; just load the wagon," and, "I was as nervous as a long-tailed cat in a room full of rocking chairs."

the intersection of Lincoln and the 10 always smell like cinnamon buns?" (I have yet to discover the source.) Another
time, I wrote: "Melon is a superfluous fruit." What on earth
would I have done if I couldn't have recorded that earth-shat-
tering insight while cruising south on Sepulveda?

These pieces of paper follow me everywhere. They're crumpled in the console of my car, wadded in the pockets of my
jackets, hibernating in the bottoms of bags next to receipts
for things I should not have bought and meant to return. The
largest heap of these notes is collecting in the corner of my
apartment where my desk meets the wall, in a formation reminiscent of a wigwam. I check occasionally to make sure a
small animal hasn't tried to make a nest inside them. I try to
contain them, with a paperweight, with a stapler, by paper-
clipping ones with similar themes together, by taping some of
my favorites to the wall, but the pile keeps growing. Some
days I'll think, okay, I'm spending today typing them into the
computer, and then I'm throwing them all away. But I can't
bring myself to do it. Because sometimes the thing it's written
on tells as much of a story as the observation itself.

Take, for example, this anecdote, written on a piece of
paper that says "Mrs. Betty Snellings" at the top and is decorated with a bluebird perched on top of a picket fence at the
bottom, red roses climbing up its sides. This is the paper my
grandmother uses to write down her grocery lists. And because this particular story is written on this particular paper,
I know exactly where I was when I wrote it: at my grandmother's house. There is a grease stain in the bottom left-hand
corner of the paper, so I remember when I wrote it, too: the
afternoon of my grandfather's funeral. The grandfather who
would say, every single time I talked to him on the phone,
"Da'lin, why do you live alllllllllll the way out in California?
Pleeeeease move back to the east, da'lin. Why don't you move
to Savannah, or Charleston, or Charlotte?" And every time,

I'd let him get all the way through his appeal, even though I already knew it by heart. For years, my grandfather pleaded with me to come back east, like it was his dying wish. When he died, I was still on the wrong coast.

After his funeral, we sat with my grandmother in her den in Georgia, eating a tin of homemade cookies, fried chicken, biscuits, green beans, and pimento cheese, drinking sweet tea during the day and cocktails at night. The following week was going to be her sixty-second wedding anniversary. All day and all night, we told stories and cried, but more than anything, we laughed. I wrote one of those stories on the grocery list paper:

■

My grandparents were driving back to Augusta after visiting some cousins in Columbus, Georgia. The whole family was in the car: my dad, who was six at the time, his older brother, and his younger sister.

"We were driving on one of those real country roads," my grandmother said. "You know Pop never liked to take the main roads." When they drove past a large factory, my grandmother said, "Look, that's where they can O'Sage Peaches."

"No, Betty," my grandfather snapped back, "That's where they can O'Sage *Pimentos*." The two of them argued passionately about this for the next four miles. "I just *knew* I had seen the word *peaches*," my grandmother said. "So I wasn't going to let it go."

Finally my grandfather got so mad he slammed on the breaks and said, "Damn it, Betty, I'm going to turn this car around and show you." And he did just that, wheeling the car in a U-turn. They rode in silence as they approached the building, each waiting to prove that they had been right. When they got to the factory, one side of the O'Sage building said, "Peaches," and the other side said, "Pimentos."

"Oh we laughed and laughed!" my grandmother said. "If only every argument could have been settled so amicably."

■

Seeing that story and her name at the top of the page reminds me of not just that day, but of many days, of all the days. It reminds me of the way my grandparents' house smelled like Joy dish soap. It reminds me where the chocolate was hidden: in the china cabinet, and if not there, then behind the Saltine cracker tin in the kitchen cupboard. It reminds me of their remote control, which they called a "clicker" and tied to the coffee table with a string so they'd never lose it. It reminds me of the collection of condiments my grandfather kept by his reclining chair—Texas Pete, Tabasco, salt, pepper, always within an arm's reach. It reminds me of the Twenty-One-Gun-Salute at his funeral, and of his flag-draped coffin. It reminds me of my brother's eulogy, perfect, without a word written down. And that reminds me of the story about the day my grandparents met:

■

My grandmother's first husband died in World War II. It's a very odd feeling, knowing that I would not be here if it weren't for that war. She was a very young widow with a very young son, my uncle Alex. My grandfather (my dad's dad) was a captain in the army and landed on Omaha Beach on D-Day Plus One. While moving inland through France, his left knee was blown out by shrapnel from an artillery shell. Most of the men around him were killed. He was evacuated to a military hospital in Augusta, Georgia, where my grandmother was volunteering as a "Grey Lady" for the American Red Cross. One of her duties as a Grey Lady was going from room to room with a basketful of items the wounded soldiers might want or need: postage stamps, pens, candy, playing cards. My grandmother was a beautiful young woman with porcelain skin and thick brown hair styled like Rita Hayworth's. When she walked into my grandfather's hospital room for the first time, he looked up from his bed, propping himself up on his elbows. She asked if he'd like anything from her basket, and my grandfather replied with a line that is as well-known in my family as our own last name: "Da'lin, what I want from you is not in that basket."

■

If the argument about the peaches and pimentos was typed into a Word Document (or the notepad app on my phone), not on my grandmother's grocery list paper with the pen she uses for crossword puzzles, and if it did not have a grease stain from the fried chicken we ate that afternoon, would it have reminded me of all of this? Would it be the same?

On the other side of that same piece of paper, I wrote down an expression my Aunt Kirkley used while listening to the story of the peaches and pimentos: "It's like being in a fork fight, and all you have is a spoon." Kirkley lives in Savannah. A flight attendant by day and a trout fisherwoman by other days, she is never short on witticisms and old-fashioned sayings. I guess I had pressed her for an explanation of this locution because I also wrote, "Oh come *on*, Lilibet, you can't stage an attack with a *spoon. Maybe* you can defend yourself. *Maybe*." Reading that, I can hear my aunt's raspy southern accent, and I can see her standing there saying it, leaning on one skinny leg, one hand gesticulating wildly, the other hand firmly gripping a Styrofoam cup full of vodka.

Numb

■

I'm sure this is hard to believe, but sometimes I forget I'm in the box. So sucked into a book, or the endless, mindless wonders of the Internet, I forget there's anyone else around. This never lasts long, though. Some body part will need rearranging—my right elbow will go numb, or the tips of my left hand will start tingling—and I'll be jolted back to reality (or, more specifically, false reality) and made aware that I am not alone, and that there is a family of four from Tallahassee twisting their necks toward me, totally confused.

Beach

∎

The box has a beach theme tonight, replete with all the appropriate accouterments: a blue beach chair with a pair of surf trunks slung over the back, three white beach towels (though they are probably hotel towels), and neon Wayfarer sunglasses. The artist has even been kind enough to include beach heat, caused by the blinding overhead lights that blast on every minute or so, the wattage of which is befitting to, say, tweezing your eyebrows, not sitting on display in your Skivvies. The concierge tells me the idea behind the schizophrenic lighting: "Now they see you, now they don't!"

All I know is they make reading and writing nauseating and are about to cause me to have a seizure. If I am going to be this hot, wearing this little clothing, I'd like to at least be getting a tan.

Because I certainly can't get one at the actual beach. That is another one of LA's secrets. Summer months by the beach are often socked in by something called a "marine layer." There's May Gray, June Gloom, and whatever other synonyms for "overcast" rhyme with "July" and "August." By the beach, summer historically shows up in September, right around the time I'm ready for it to be over. Cruelly, the marine layer only happens by the ocean; inland LA is clear and hot all summer long. Whenever my friends who live east would talk about driving to Venice Beach, I'd suggest I drive inland instead, and we'd sit on their rooftops.

Here's another dirty secret: the beaches in LA are not very nice. Sure, north of LA and south of LA—in Malibu or Manhattan Beach, say—they are gorgeous, but not so much in Santa Monica or Venice. One afternoon, while I was at the beach in Venice, my sunbathing was interrupted with a tap on my shoulder.

"Excuse me?" a high-pitched man's voice said. "Do you know what time it is?"

I shaded the sun with my hand and looked up. A man in a Speedo hovered above me.

"2:58."

"Oh thank you," he said, and then he just stood there. I glanced up again and realized this man was also wearing a bikini top and makeup that must have been applied in the dark.

"My name is Tammy," he said. "Sometimes I cross-dress but I think I look pretty good. How do you think I look?"

"You look great." I said, flatly.

"Oh, really? That's so nice."

I focused my eyes back on my book, hoping he'd go away. Instead, he plopped down beside me, stretched out, and fell asleep.

Once I felt confident he was asleep and not dead, I gathered my things and folded up my chair. That was about all I could stand for one day.

I have noticed, however, that if someone asks what I did that day and I say I spent the day at the beach, they'll often say something like, "Nice!" or "Good for you!" But if someone asked what I did that day and I said, "Oh I just laid on my floor, read *Us Weekly*, and ate a bag of potato chips," no one is going to congratulate me. But it's basically the same thing. At least in my apartment I don't have to contend with skin cancer, sand, or cross-dressers named Tammy.

Voyeur

∎

This term has become so overused, it seems to have lost all relation to its original meaning. In its original definition, a voyeur is "one obtaining sexual gratification from observing unsuspecting individuals who are partly undressed, naked, or engaged in sexual acts." Perhaps as a result of its overuse, a second definition has been added: "A prying observer who is usually seeking the sordid or the scandalous."

The word *voyeur* is French for "one who sees." Thus, the sexual undertones are not surprising; with the French, it seems, everything is sexual. Over time, the definition has shifted, and those sexual connotations have, for the most part, been lost. What has also been lost is the word "unsuspecting." In the original definition, the person being viewed is unaware that anyone is looking.

Voyeurism in the modern context, however, seems to imply the watched are acutely mindful of being watched. Be it a participant on a reality show, an online exhibitionist who posts videos of her daily doings, or the everyday Facebook user, the individuals being viewed are now hyperconscious of their audience.

Reality show stars sometimes claim they "forget" the camera is rolling. There is no way they forget. From my very limited experience with taping reality TV, I can assure you, there is no way they forget. One of the models I had represented asked me to participate in a shoot for her reality show pilot. (The show never got picked up.) For the episode, I was going to be the "friend at the coffee shop." To be fair, she and I were actually friends in real life. Before we shot the scene, the producers held me in my car so our "Hellos!" and "So good to see yous!" would seem genuine. Those initial pleasantries were the only remotely real part of the whole process. The director would interrupt every minute or so to re-direct our conversation. He told me what questions to ask, such as, "What did your boyfriend's parents think about you doing *Playboy*?" This question wasn't exactly off the top of my head, considering I had completely forgotten that she had ever even been in *Playboy*, but I guess "Where did you buy that sweater?" didn't make for interesting television.

On a smaller, more routine scale, we willingly—eagerly, even—hand over infinite amounts of personal information to the loosest of acquaintances, to non-acquaintances, to strangers. This is voluntary. We sign up to do this. We log on to do this. (By "we" I mean everyday users and consumers of social media. By "we" I mean me, because I am guilty of all of this.)

We trade our privacy for that connection, that validation we crave. In a lot of ways, I think our obsession with watching other people has more to do with us wanting to believe that we are also worth watching. If someone else doesn't see what we've done—that piece we published, or that picture from the party last night—it disappears. Memories no longer suffice; moments must be made concrete, made real through photos posted on the Internet.

Hyper-aware of being watched, we tailor our online behaviors to present the version of ourselves that we believe (or
wish) ourselves to be. There are two strands at work here: the
public versus the private self, and the person versus the per-
sona. There is the person living the life, then the same person
mastering how their puppet appears. We are the art directors
of our online lives.

Sadly, it sometimes seems our online selves are outpacing
our real selves. I see many of my friends on Instagram more
than I see them in real life. A friend told me that, at a wedding
recently, one of the groomsmen grabbed the microphone on
the bus to the reception and said, "I think we all know what
we are here to do: drink beer and Instagram."

I often find myself initiating conversations and getting
cut off mid-anecdote. "Yeah I saw that," someone will say.
They've already seen the pictures on Instagram or Facebook,
or they've read something about it on Twitter. I hate leading
with, "I don't know if you saw this, but . . ." because I don't
like making the assumption that everyone sees everything I've
ever posted online. At the same time, I also live in constant
fear of repeating myself. It's not easy to navigate between the
moments for which we are present and the moments we are
recording.

While I'm sure the box concept was more radical when it
was built in 1998, I think it's more relevant now, as our obsession with watching other people live their lives has reached an
almost-predatory level. The box is supposed to be the physical
embodiment of this obsession, of watching someone live her
life. It's supposed to be voyeuristic. But with the emergence
of the Internet, this concept seems dated. And perhaps, in a
quaint way, that's what makes the box even more interesting
today than it was in 1998. Maybe in this age of over-sharing,
that's its most unique asset. A voyeur can see some stuff, but
not all your stuff. And unlike on Facebook or Instagram or

anywhere else on the Internet, I am incapable of over-sharing. If anything, I'm under-sharing. Leaving something to the imagination. Someone can Google far more information about any person on the planet than anyone standing fifteen feet away can find out about me.

True Facts About a Box Girl[9]

1. I hope that someday my best girlfriends and I outlive our husbands so we can move to Miami and live like *The Golden Girls*.
2. I have never met a Gemini, a Canadian, or a person from Maryland I don't like.
3. By some freak chance, I won a free throw contest in the fourth grade by making nine out of ten baskets. My picture was in the local paper. (Small town; it must have been a slow week for rabid raccoon sightings.)
4. I once drove off with the gas nozzle still stuck in my car; ripped the thing right off the pump. There are conflicting theories as to whose fault this actually was. There are three potential suspects: Me because I was driving the car; Rachel because she was pumping the gas; and Heather because she accidentally forgot to pay for her bag of chips inside the gas station. The prevailing theory is that it was Heather's fault because of karma and all.

---

9 I am aware that "true fact" is redundant.

5. In college, I once drank an entire bottle of hot sauce for $500. Under no circumstances do I suggest doing this. I wasn't right for weeks.

6. Heather and I used to have a pet goldfish named Tuna, but not for very long. Apparently we were feeding him too much food because he popped. Literally exploded. There were bits of poor Tuna all over that fishbowl.

7. I have always wanted to know: Who put the cat *in* the bag?

8. I want to know what the hell ever happened to The Food Pyramid, when I was *encouraged* to eat six to eleven servings of bread a day.

9. When I was a child, I used to find it wildly amusing when my older brother would pretend he was retarded in public places, and, at say, Toys"R"Us, would throw himself on the ground screaming and flailing around until my mom couldn't take it anymore and would grab him by the arm and yell, "Get up! Get up, damnit!" and strangers would be like, "Oh what a horrible mother treating her retarded son like that." He was really good at this.

10. I am sorry if the above offended anyone. Now that I am closer to child-rearing age and have friends with special-needs children, this isn't that funny anymore. But man, in 1989, this was pee-in-your-pants hilarious.

11. I am terrified of what kids can do on computers these days. I don't trust anyone under twelve.

12. I have no idea how the Internet works. I would love for someone to explain it to me. Until someone does, I am going to accept "magic" as the explanation.

13. I have no idea how dry cleaning works. I believe that, too, is magical. I don't care for an explanation.

14. My personal purgatory would be looking for my car in a never-ending parking garage with John Mayer's "Your Body Is a Wonderland" playing on a loop.

15. I hope heaven is a giant breakfast buffet.

Sometimes I Wish
a Blackberry Was Still Just a Fruit

> In the pre-Internet age . . . there came a moment when you
> turned off the TV or the stereo, or put down the book or mag-
> azine . . . You stopped doing culture and you withdrew—or
> advanced—into your solitude. You used the phone. You went
> for a walk. You went to the corner bar for a drink. You made
> love . . . You wrote a letter.
>
> —Lee Siegel, *Against The Machine*

It is important to understand that I am the sort of button-fearing technophobe who, given the choice of figuring out how to use someone else's remote control or staring at a wall and picking at my fingernails, will invariably go with the latter. Thus, iPhones were my worst nightmare. It's like an airplane cockpit with all those buttons. One mis-touch and I might prematurely eject the landing gear. When I lamented this to a friend, he said, "Actually, the iPhone doesn't have any buttons." Whatever they are—buttons, magical touch-screen non-buttons—I don't care.

I didn't want a phone that was smarter than me. I just wanted a simple, relatively portable contraption that would make calls, send texts, and give me my email. For many years, that device was my Blackberry. I loved my Blackberry, so sturdy and dependable. If it were a human, its name would have been Steve. It never dropped calls—not even in elevators or parking garages—and was built like a Sherman tank.

Steve was dropped, stepped on, and drowned on more occasions than I can count. Many times, after it slipped from my grip mid-conversation, I'd watch proudly as it did a double backflip, with a twist, and stuck the landing. Then I'd simply pick it up, brush off the dirt, and continue my conversation.

I'm not sure Steve appreciated the abuse, though. After it landed in my toilet twice in one month, I decided it might be trying to tell me something. While the first time was an accident—it fell from my sweatshirt's front pocket while I was cleaning the bathroom—the second time was clearly an act of suicide: It vibrated itself right off the ledge.

My relationship with cellular technology was rocky right out of the gates. In college, on one of my first trips to the Verizon store, I managed to get into two car accidents in five minutes. I hit a patch of ice in the parking lot and rammed into the back of a parked truck, and as I pleaded with the mountain man in the truck, a mom in an SUV hit the same patch of ice and slammed into my car's rear end. Two fender-benders later, I still hadn't gotten my cell phone taken care of, which had also been the victim of a recent accident. (This one involved being dropped into a Solo cup.) The salesperson at Verizon would only give me a new phone if I promised to keep it in a jazzy black leather case. "You can clip it to your belt" was actually one of the selling points.

The truth is, back then it didn't really matter if there was an embarrassing leather case holstering my phone because no matter how hard I tried to buy a "cool" cell phone, I always ended up with something huge and blue. Melissa told me one of my phones looked like a giant blue nose. I diligently kept it hidden in my purse and, when its public use was absolutely necessary, buried it under my hair while talking. When someone would say, "Let me put my number in your phone," I pretended I didn't have it with me.

"Oh I'll just jot it down the old-fashioned way on this Dentyne wrapper," I'd say. Invariably, at that very moment, the blue nose would start ringing, and I would have to reveal it. "What do you know?" I'd say, digging through my purse. "It's in here!"

During a summer internship in 2003, when my boss asked me to pick up his Blackberry, I thought he was talking about a muffin. How could I have predicted that, ten years later, the word "blackberry" would no longer conjure images of homemade preserves, the term "cell phone" would be considered passé, and technology would have essentially taken over our lives?

In 2006, I wrote a magazine article about a guy who directed movies shot specifically for viewing on a cell phone. I sat there, bulbous blue flip phone with a Nintendo-green screen vibrating in my purse, and said, "You've got to be kidding me." He wasn't kidding me. The opening paragraph of that article read, "Movies on your cell phone? Really???" I wasn't trying to be ironic. I honesty could not fathom watching a movie on a phone. "But the screen is so small," I objected, during the interview. "Why would anyone do that when they have a TV?" I asked.

When I started working in the box in 2007, I had the aforementioned blue flip phone and a Hewlett Packard laptop, which weighed approximately one hundred pounds. Since then, the evolution of the electronic devices that have joined me in the box is as follows:

Blue flip phone
Hewlett Packard laptop

iPod: giant, white, with the gray, Apple II-E font and the
click wheel
White Apple MacBook
Blackberry: all black with the scrolling wheel on the side
iPod Mini: green, still with gray-and-white screen
Blackberry: silver and black, the side scrolling wheel
replaced by a center scrolling ball
Kindle: white, second-generation
Silver Apple MacBook Pro
Blackberry: black, with the flat, touch-sensitive scrolling
pad
iPod Nano: square-shaped, black, color screen
iPad: black, first-generation, hand-me-down from Peter
iPhone 4

My dad once sent a blast email to the family, announcing,
Not to worry everybody; he'd reserved a Gmail address for his
grandson, my nephew. He was six months old.

By eighteen months, that same nephew thought a golden
retriever named Ace lived inside the computer because he so
often Skyped with his other aunt and her dog. By two, he had
his own iPad, which was covered in dinosaur stickers. He knew
how to swipe to unlock it, select the icon of his favorite game,
and play. I watched in awe one Christmas as he stood over his
iPad, his fat, alligator arms masterfully swooshing across the
screen like a painter over his palette. It was impressive. And
intimidating. I did not, at the time, know how to do this.

Sometimes I dream about the days before Facebook and
G-chat, before Instagram and iPhones. Before iPads and iEv-
erything. Back when an Apple was still an apple, The Cloud
was just a cloud, and Siri was just the misspelled name of Tom
Cruise's daughter. Back before Twitter and Tumblr, and before
phone conversations were so taboo. Before texting and not
talking & abbrvting everything. Back when OMG and WTF

were just someone's initials. Back when Thursday was not #tbt, and we did not LOL at our own jokes. Back when we were forced to pick up the phone because we didn't know who was calling.

Sometimes I am nostalgic for the '90s. Back when I thought "The Internet" and "America Online" were the same thing. Back when I could actually figure out how to operate a remote control—Power, Channel Up/Down, Volume Up/Down. There was still TV on TV, music on MTV, and *The Real World* was the only reality show in town. Flannels were cool for the first time—worn open, with a T-shirt. Rappers didn't want to be anybody's role model, and the only kid in high school who had a cell phone was the kid who sold weed. And even then, it was probably a pager, not a cell phone.

That was back when you had to drive into town to find out what your friends were up to. Back when you never knew who you were going to run into. Back when you were only concerned with living the moment, not documenting yourself living the moment.

It was a time, for me, of heady naiveté and fierce metabolism, when cellulite was something only old ladies had, terrorism was something only in faraway, hard-to-pronounce countries (or Will Smith movies) and the term *recession* was some abstract concept I learned about in Social Studies class, something that sounded about as likely to someday affect me as The Potato Famine.

■

After my Blackberry killed itself, I considered not replacing it out of respect. Like when a beloved family dog dies. I also contemplated following in my dad's contrarian footsteps. He has never owned a cell phone in his life, and this never ceases to impress me. He is a very hard man to get a hold of. People call him at home, and if he's not at home, then they don't get to talk to him.

I knew I'd never do it, though, as much as I was dying for one of those old-school answering machines with the mini cassette tapes. (What would my outgoing message be? Would I do the one where I pretend I answer? Maybe sing a song? The options were endless.) I thought about getting another Blackberry, but it was getting kind of embarrassing. Plus, my mom had gotten an iPhone. I'd been leapfrogged. After much agonizing, I finally capitulated: an iPhone it was. Before I left the house, I hugged my waterlogged Blackberry goodbye. "It's been a good run, Steve," I said, and threw him in the garbage can.

I took a moment to psych myself up for the dreaded trip to the Apple store. As if Apple stores are not terrifying enough, the only one within miles of my apartment was located on the Third Street Promenade, in Santa Monica, a pedestrian shopping mall teeming with tourists in Tevas and teenagers making out in front of movie theaters. I decided I'd make the trip in the mid-afternoon, while everyone else was at work. What I forgot was that LA doesn't host a traditional workday. It took me almost an hour to find a parking spot. I wanted to kill myself before I even got into the store.

When I finally got my hands on an iPhone, my fingers fumbled. I just didn't have that deft, touch-screen touch. It was like André the Giant attempting to needlepoint a purse. Poking bluntly at its lack of buttons, I asked one of the employees if there was an instruction manual. He shuddered a bit. "Oh, it doesn't have an instruction manual," he said. "We just encourage people to play around with it to learn." What a load of crap. My *toaster* has an instruction manual.

Eventually making my escape, iPhone in hand, the first text came from Peter, forever the Monday morning quarterback: "You know you could have just gone to the Verizon store, right?" I would have liked to write back: "Thanks for telling me after I spent two traumatizing hours in the Apple store." But all my bumbling little fingers could muster was: "Shit."

To use a phrase from the '90s, let's fast-forward a few days. I'm sitting in the box, cradling my iPhone like a beautiful baby bird, stroking and swiping its angelic little feathers. I coo at it like a newborn baby. "How did I ever live without you, you sleek and brilliant thing?" I whisper to it. "What a wonderful addition to my life in the box you will be." It's just so hand-held, like my own mini computer! Now I don't have to be hunched over my laptop to surf the web. All of this stuff, right at my fingertips! No, it's not quite as easy to navigate as a toaster, but it's a lot more intuitive than a remote control.

I will forever have a soft spot for the '90s, remembering envelopes, phones with cords, before infants had email addresses. But I don't think it's the absence of technology that draws me to that decade. I think what I really miss is the certainty and the security, even in my naiveté. It was a moment in my personal history when I felt impervious to all things bad. When I could pull the covers over my head and sleep soundly, knowing that we were all going to be safe.

The Big One

■

The front pane of glass shakes. I *knew* there would be an earthquake while I was in the box. As with most situations that require me to take some sort of action, I freeze. I have neither fight nor flight: I just stand there, dumfounded, like a kid who just peed in his pants.

I'm going to be buried alive in a pile of concrete and glass while sitting in the box. What a way to go. I can see His Majesty now, manning the pearly gates with a clipboard and a headset, like a bouncer at a nightclub, making his final judgments. "Well," he'll say, giving me the old holier-than-thou once-over as only He can do, "Based on *that* getup, I think we're gonna have to redirect you downstairs for reassignment—*way* downstairs."

I finally look up. I was wrong. It's not an earthquake at all. It's the concierge. He's cleaning the glass with paper towels and Windex. I should point out that he is doing this very aggressively. Does he have any idea how startling that is in here? Is he trying to hurt the glass? This guy's a little firecracker, bald and compact. He stands at his computer with his legs far apart, like a football coach, or a male cheerleader. Next to his computer is a hot coffee with a straw, and beside that, a pack of Parliament Lights.

Since I took my first steps into California, I have been certain The Big One will come for us at any minute. Because of this, I am constantly hatching disaster preparedness plans. Every building I enter is assessed for structural soundness, and the first thing I do when I walk into a room is survey the furniture to determine the safest place to hunker down. I always move my water glass away from my laptop whenever I step away from it, for even a minute, and I will never go more than one floor below ground level in a parking garage.

My neurosis about natural disasters no doubt has something to do with my dad, who fancies himself something of a recreational meteorologist. He is fascinated by weather and other terrifying natural phenomena. In college, he used to tell me I needed to drive up to Yellowstone "before she blows." He would remind me, "It's not an 'if,' it's a 'when.'" This wasn't particularly comforting considering I went to school only five hundred miles south of there. "Oh, that wouldn't matter," he'd say, and I'd feel momentarily relieved. "If she blows, it would be the end of mankind as we know it."

I called my parents after I heard an asteroid the size of an aircraft carrier was supposed to hit Earth later that day. Not supposed to, but could have. It was closer than any other asteroid since 1976—only two hundred thousand miles away. The "Near Earth Objects Scientist" who was being interviewed on NPR said if it hit land, it would take out all of Los Angeles, and if it hit sea, it would create two-hundred-foot waves. Either way, in the words of our former governor, "Hasta la vista, baby."

My mom answered the phone as I merged onto the 105 East. "Did you hear about this asteroid that's supposed to hit earth today?" I asked.

"No! What?" She then shouted, "Bill! Have you heard about this asteroid that's supposed to hit earth today?"

I waited a moment for her to come back to the receiver. "Your father just smirked and said we've got at least another hour."

"Put him on the phone," I said. "Dad, what do you mean? It's not supposed to hit us, is it?"

"Well," he said. "If our scientists are worth a damn then it's not. But I'm enjoying a stiff Stoli martini right now just in case they're wrong."

Shortly after, I had a nightmare about an earthquake. The world was swaying from side to side, like a cruise ship righting itself just before it capsizes. I was sliding from one end of a mall to the other. Everyone was slipping toward Nordstrom, then slamming back against Bloomingdale's. Somehow, I got out of the mall and climbed a cliff with a waterfall. (I don't know; it was a dream.) At the top of the waterfall, there was a room. I tried to get under a table, but before I could, I was thrown to the other side of the room and ejected out a window, into the sunny LA sky. I flew along the coast, over beautiful beachfront houses, some on fire, and everyone below me was clinging onto something—a mailbox, a tree trunk, a telephone pole—so they didn't get thrown into the air like me. This sort of dream is not uncommon for me. I only have one recurring nightmare, always from the apocalyptic genre.

∎

The glass rattles again. This time, the Firecracker Concierge falls backward and bangs into it. I really wish he would stop. Between the nightmare and a strange, out-of-place earthquake on the East Coast, I've been jumpier than usual.

The earthquake on the East Coast hadn't even stopped trembling when my mom called me, carrying on as if the world was coming to an end. She was at the Theta House at Yale, of all places, where she is the housemother (seriously), and was helping the girls move in for the fall semester. She said Thetas were screaming and scattering everywhere.

"Don't worry, ya'll!" she announced after the tremors, "I'll call my daughter in California!"

When she called, she asked, "Now if there's an aftershock, should we get in the basement?"

"The basement! God, no!" I said.

"No Betty, the bathtub!" one of the girls shouted.

"No, not the bathtub," I said. "That is for hurricanes and tornadoes. You've got your natural disasters all mixed up."

Ivy League or not, these East Coast women had absolutely no idea what to do with an earthquake.

"Get under a table," I told her.

"We don't have any tables yet!" my mom said, and then she shouted to the other housemother, "Carol, we need to get that dining room table, *now*."

Then my mom said she had to get off the phone because she had to go buy a table.

■

Because of my illogical and unrelenting fear of where I will be when The Big One hits, I typically spend a few moments each shift deciding what I would do in the event of an earthquake striking while I am in the box. The most serious problem is, of course, that I'm surrounded by glass. I've decided crawling under the mattress is my best bet, but based upon my reflexes tonight, I'm sure I'd probably just lie there and wait for the shards of glass to kill me.

One month, this fear was particularly pronounced be-cause the back wall of the box was covered in little porcelain plates—twenty-six of them. I counted.

Prickly leaves and pastel roses adorned each of the twenty-six darling plates, the edges of which were scalloped and delicately rimmed in gold. I wished I could have flipped them over to see what pattern they were, but they were stuck to the wall. (I tried.) They looked like they once lived in my grandmother's breakfront, removed from their protective cases only for the finer meals. In the front of the box were Lucite boxes filled with even more dinner plates, those ones smashed into big chunks. There were a dozen or so different patterns—I didn't take an exact count of those. I recognized at least two of the patterns. My mom collects the green ones that look like leaves. They're called Majolica, she told me. They have the veiny, lumpy texture of a fern frond. I also recognized the blue-and-white Chinese-looking plates. Those ornate numbers with a picture of a pagoda, two doves, and an apple tree are Blue Willow. My mom doesn't use those for eating, though—they are hung in a cluster on her kitchen wall, for decoration. Then, most terrifyingly, there was a glass box full of plate shards mounted to the wall, right above my head.

I'm actually not sure which would be worse during an earthquake—the box or my apartment in Venice, which is certain to collapse like a house of flimsy, worn-out cards, the ones that are hard to shuffle. The only thing I am sure of is this: In the event of The Big One, the absolute last place I want to be is among the library book stacks at the University of Southern California. While it is one of the most beautiful college libraries in the country, if you happen to find yourself in those book stacks during The Big One, well, it's been a good run.

The first time I ventured into these stacks I was in search of three titles, which I had scribbled on the back of a Coffee Bean receipt. A librarian turned to his computer and told me they didn't have two of the books but one of them was "down there." Awkwardly gripping a tiny, eraser-less pencil, he hunched over a square of scrap paper and wrote down

the call number: "PS355305789z46252006." (I'm not kidding, that was it. Of course I still have the piece of paper.) He
said it was on Floor Two, so I'd have to go down four floors.
Down four floors? *Aren't I on floor one?* I thought. *Is two not
above one?*

"Have you ever been down there?" he asked.

"No," I said.

Why did he keep referring to it as "down there"?

He handed me a detailed yet entirely incomprehensible
map, which he said needed to be returned when I got "back
up." Was I going spelunking? Did I need a headlamp? An ava-
lanche beacon? What the hell was going on here?

Armed with my map (which I immediately gave up using
for its intended purpose and started using as a fan), I began
my expedition to the inner bowels of the beast. *How far below
ground level is Floor Two,* I thought. *Will I hit water? Uncover
a lost treasure? Capture a troll?*

Below me, taped firmly to the floor, was a path in the shape
of stacked arrows, in a color I can only call emergency red.
Laced with hot pink, it was a more panicked version of regular red, which said not just, "Follow me to the nearest exit,"
but, "Drop your shit and sprint." I followed these arrows to
an archaic elevator, where I half expected an attendant to be
standing inside—top hat, gloves, and all—cranking a lever to
deliver me to my destination.

As I emerged from the elevator, I actually laughed. The
stacks of books went on as far as I could see, in every direction, so tall and narrow and close together that, when standing
with my hands on my hips, both elbows touched book spines.
My journey began in section PQ1643: French, Italian, Spanish,
and Portuguese Literature; an ocean away from where I
wanted to be. While the initial effect of this literary catacomb
was dizzying, the smell was heavenly—the dusty, sour-milk-
and-starch stench of old books.

The books went on forever—books of poems, books of plays, an entire section of books of quotations: *The Quotable Woman, Who Said What In 1971, What Great Men Say About Other Great Men.* I began to get lost in the titles, pulling out intriguing ones, stopping, sitting, starting again. Before I knew it, I had an armful of books, none on my original list.

Though the setting was ideal for a psychological thriller, I didn't want to leave. It was so quiet and set apart. My own little underground world. I stopped in front of a book I'd always wanted to read and slid down the side of the stacks onto the floor. An hour went by. Maybe a day? A chair scratched against the floor above me, and I looked up. Neon white lights buzzed overhead, and the shelves, towering almost to the ceiling, were loaded with heavy, hardbound books. I took a picture from below and send it to Peter with a caption that said, "I hope there's not an earthquake." But the text wouldn't send. My Blackberry signal said "SOS," no one in, no one out.

I began picturing my demise. The ground would start to shake, and the lights would swing overhead, some snapping in half. Shelves would fall like dominoes, one onto another, books crashing below. I'd be huddled there, hands-over-head, in the American Lit section, trapped between H.L. Mencken, J.D. Salinger, and other writers who were already dead. The final blow would come from above: At 1,285 pages, Norman Mailer's *The Time of Our Time* would be the end of me.

■

The Firecracker Concierge falls into the glass again. What is the deal? Is this guy drunk? Now the deejay is leaning against the glass. These people obviously don't know how alarming this is. I eye the pane of glass above me, wondering how, exactly, it would shatter.

Tsunami

I recently got a notice in the mail, outlining the tsunami danger zones for coastal Los Angeles. I looked for my street. It was highlighted in purple. Purple seemed good. Purple was not red. Purple was not orange. Purple was not even yellow. What could purple possibly mean? I read the legend. Next to purple it said: "Tsunami Inundation Zone." As if my garage apartment was not scary enough. *Maybe I should start sleeping on a raft,* I thought. With a helmet, and rain boots, and a life jacket, and a paddle.

According to the pamphlet, because I am in the "Inundation Zone," I am encouraged to get the hell out of there as soon as an earthquake stops quaking. It suggests I head for higher ground on foot, because there will probably be all sorts of crap in the streets. (I'm paraphrasing.) My most recent tsunami escape plan is to wait out the shaking in my bathroom doorway, because it's the only interior doorway, and I think my twee Parisian café table, however darling and shabby chic, won't suffice as a barrier between my head and falling objects. After the trembling subsides, I'll put on a pair of running shoes, then grab a jacket, my purse, my laptop, and a box of cereal. Armed with my Multi Grain Cheerios, I will make my escape.

I almost executed this plan one night when I was awakened by a friend who told me to turn on the news. A magnitude 8.9 earthquake had just hit the coast of Japan, and a tsunami was headed our way. I don't know if it was my friend's panicked voice jolting me awake, or the doomsday music on CNN, but I was positive we were done for. I called Peter (we didn't yet live together) and told him, in my most authoritative voice, that we needed to head for higher ground.

"Huh?" he said, his voice thick with sleep.

"There's been an 8.9 earthquake in Japan, and there's a tsunami warning for the coast of California," I said.

"Huh?" he repeated.

I repeated myself, more urgently this time.

"Is Wolf Blitzer awake?" he said.

"Huh?" I said.

"Is Wolf Blitzer awake?" he repeated.

"No. It's some guy I don't know," I said.

"Call me if Wolf Blitzer wakes up," he said, then let out a loud yawn.

"But who cares if it's Wolf Blitzer or not? They are playing the doomsday music!"

"Has it hit Hawaii?"

"Has what hit Hawaii?"

"The tsunami. Has it hit Hawaii?"

"No," I said.

"Call me when it hits Hawaii," he said, "That should give us at least six hours."

■

A friend of mine was staying in Hawaii that night at a fancy hotel. She said they moved everyone onto the golf course—the highest point on the hotel's property. They pitched tents and set out silver buffet trays of food. A string quartet played, she said, to calm everyone's nerves, "Like in the final moments of the Titanic."

The tsunami never hit Hawaii. Or at least, not very hard. It never hit the continental United States, either. Actually, that's not true. I think a boat was overturned in Oregon.

Scotch Please, Splash Soda

My parents are now "snowbirds," meaning they fly south in the winter for a warmer climate. They spend six months on the coast of southern Georgia and six months in the hills of southern Connecticut, which allows my dad to play golf in near-perfect conditions all year long.

My parents' Georgia home is a picture of Southern hospitality. Most every surface is monogrammed—the bath towels, the coasters, the seashell-shaped soaps. Give a WASPy Southern woman a millimeter of material, and she'll figure out a way to put someone's initials on it. During the holidays, the monogrammed cocktail napkins are replaced by a stack of green ones that say, "Holidays with the family are always a trip. A trip to the liquor store." I think these napkins were created with my family in mind. As my grandmother once said, elbow-deep in a Scotch and soda, "Jews don't recognize Jesus as the Messiah. Protestants don't recognize the Pope as the head of the church. Baptists don't recognize each other at the liquor store." We're not Baptists, but based on my family's idolatrous worship of alcohol, we might as well be.

While most children spend the week before Christmas shopping and wrapping, I prepare by resting, hydrating, and stretching. You have to understand, these people are animals. And by animals, I mean my grandfather, my grandmothers, and my great-aunt, all in their late eighties or early nineties. If these folks don't have a drink in hand by four o'clock, they rattle their canes in protest. And they only drink the hard stuff, or "meaningful drinks," as my dad calls them: bourbon and water, Scotch and soda, gin and tonic, vodka on the rocks, the occasional Bloody Mary (but only if it's before noon), and wine (but only if it's with dinner). If there's one thing upstanding Southern WASPs like to do to celebrate the birth of Christ, it's get drunk.

The location for this bourbon-soaked soiree is Sea Island, Georgia, an emerald enclave of the rich and retired, covered in golf courses, spas, and Spanish moss, where money hangs from the Magnolia trees. While waiting tables one night, a customer said, "*Wait*, your parents live in *Sea Island*? Why the hell are you working as a *waitress*?" It's that sort of place.

At the helm of this holiday operation is my mom, a perky perfectionist who was once crowned The Sweetheart of Sigma Chi at The University of Georgia, and the Miss Augusta *runner-up* (but we wont talk about that). Christmas gives her an excuse to be in a great mood at 7:00 am, shower people with presents, decorate and re-decorate, and drink in the afternoon. So hopped up on the holidays, she didn't even notice one year when I wrapped a cashmere sweater I had borrowed from her two years prior. "Oh I just *love* this," she said, swirling a celery stalk into her Bloody Mary. "And it's *just* my color."

My mom desperately wants us to share her zeal for the holidays. One Easter, she wanted her children—ages twenty-nine and twenty-six at the time—to participate in an egg hunt, so she stuffed the plastic pastel eggs full of money. Sitting on the patio, hungover, sweating, hands shaking, her "children" were barely breathing, let alone showing any interest in skipping around the yard for eggs. Finally, she yelled, "Damn it, y'all, there's money in them!" Some eggs had singles, some fives, others tens and twenties. My brother and I tore toward the lawn. After several slide tackles and a yellow-card's worth of elbowing each other in the ribs, our knees skinned and covered in grass stains, my mom got just what she wanted: joyful holiday togetherness.

My mom never turns down an invitation, certainly not at Christmas. Every year on Christmas Eve, she insists we go to this god-awful caroling and Yule-log-lighting party, and she drags the entire geriatric wing of the family along. But they don't seem to mind. After all, these bloodhounds can smell eggnog from a mile away.

My least favorite of our holiday traditions is the dreaded staging of The Christmas Card Picture. While this was a perfectly acceptable tradition when my brother and I were kids, now that we're adults, it's just plain embarrassing. At least for me. My brother now has a wife and two children, so in our Christmas Card Picture it's very obvious that there's: 1) an older couple in their sixties, 2) a cute young married couple in their thirties with two darling little boys, and 3) shoved somewhere in the periphery, me.

I am sure the four-hundred-plus recipients of the annual card must wonder:

"Is she still single?"

"She must be a lesbian."

"Betty with a lesbian daughter, no."

"But she does live in California."

"And I think she worked for the Obama campaign."

One year, after the cards were delivered, my mom got an email from a friend in Texas: "Just wanted to say I'm so happy to see that Lilibet is expecting!" My mom called me immediately, horrified. I ripped the thing off my fridge.

"Oh my god," I said, "I *do* look pregnant." Something had gone horribly wrong with the lighting, the angle, something. We discussed, in disbelief, for the next hour.

"See, she was the only one to *say* something," my mom said. "I wonder how many people thought it but didn't say anything? I mean, my Lord, do these people actually think I'd put you in the picture pregnant *with no husband?*"

■

At the other end of the holiday jolliness spectrum—the very other end—is my dad. He sees Christmas as nothing but one giant MasterCard bill. *Bah humbug* doesn't even do it justice. Perhaps bah hum—*to hell with these damn Christmas lights, why don't we have any vermouth, damn it Betty if I have to listen to that damn Rod Stuart Christmas CD one more time*—bug.

This is, after all, a man who prefers funerals to weddings, because they're less expensive to attend. "*And* you don't have to hang around afterward and mingle," he said to me one day. "No gift, no tux, no dancing, just a quick in and out." I listened, brow-furrowed and eyes bulging.

"Yeah, but someone died," I said.

He bulldozed on. "It's a much more tasteful affair, much more courteous to the guests if you ask me."

My mom and dad fill each other's stockings. My mom buys my dad practical items, things he likes or uses: toothpaste, Altoids, a bag of pistachios. My mom's stocking is always a cornucopia of used objects my dad picked up around the house: a can opener, an ice cream scooper, a half-eaten banana.

My dad hates getting presents and typically responds with "How much did this cost me?" instead of "Thank you." That is, unless he really wants something. Then he buys it for himself, wraps it, and signs the card: "To Bill, Love Kiki." Kiki is his imaginary girlfriend, and he thinks this is hilarious. Kiki has given him every club in his golf bag.

The only presents my dad does like are ones that don't cost any money. When I ran cross-country at the University of Colorado and my brother played golf at the University of North Carolina, my dad received every possible university-logoed item: socks, hats, shoes, T-shirts, golf balls, women's-sized shoes. He didn't care, as long as it was free. When I worked at the agency, I raided the supply room for gifts. That year he got boxes of pens, staples, paper clips, a bundle of highlighters. I've never seen him so proud.

While my brother is more willing to spend money on presents, he never purchases any of them until the day before. "I'm just headed out to get a coffee," he'll say, meaning: "I'm going to the shopping center down the street to buy all of your presents." Fortunately, there's a bookstore, but aside from books, his presents are useless. Over the years, he has given me a George Foreman grill (how was I going to get it back to California?), a Slap Chop ("As seen on TV!"), foot cream, and a pair of men's socks. His last-minute wrapping jobs are a vision as well: always an abstract experiment in torn paper and Scotch Tape. (I don't think he's ever used scissors.) Selfishly, I like it when he lacks creativity and just gives me money. This, however, is never your standard affair. One year he wrapped up a crumpled handful of bills—whatever was on top of his dresser, I'm sure. It totaled sixty-eight dollars. The card read: "Dear Lilibet, I hope this helps get you back above the poverty line."

My extended family is not into traditional gifts, either. Since I was sixteen, my Uncle Ross, who is also my godfather, has given me liquor for Christmas: a bottle of pink champagne, some fruit-flavored vodka. Because the rest of the family started getting jealous, Uncle Ross now arrives each Christmas with a cardboard box full of booze—sometimes the bottles are wrapped, sometimes not—and hands them out like Santa Claus (or maybe like a fake Mall Santa who has a drinking problem): Scotch for my dad, some obscure beer for my brother, a bottle of merlot for my mom.

My Aunt Kirkley is also known for her gag gifts, though it's hard to call them "gag" because all of her presents fall under this category. Because she is a flight attendant, I think she buys most of her presents at the airport. My last gift from her was a solar-powered clock in the shape of a sunflower, which bobs its head and flaps its leaves when exposed to direct sunlight.

A friend asked my dad one year if we had any Christmas Day traditions, like playing a game of flag football. (I guess this is what The Kennedys did.) My dad thought about it for a minute, then replied, "No, we generally just sit around, drink Bloody Marys, and insult each other." I come from a long line of wise-asses. Being funny is a must with this group. Everyone is always trying to outwit one another with the notes on their gift tags, and the more absurd the present, the better. The worst wrapping job wins.

■

Sitting around the dining room table for supper on Christmas afternoons, my dad will say, "Cheers," clinking a spoon against his wine glass. "To your mother, who managed to only burn *two* of the five casseroles this year." I'll look around the table. Yet again, my mom has found a way to put pecans in every single dish. Somehow, every year, she manages to forget that her daughter is deathly, gone-to-the-emergency-room-four-times allergic to nuts. My grandmother refuses to believe this. "That is just the *wildest* thing I've ever heard," she'll say, heaping a giant piece of pecan pie on my plate. Picking at the crust, I'll decide the only way to avoid anaphylaxis is to drink my dinner. So I'll dive nose first into a glass of Cabernet so large, a small bird could bathe in it.

An hour later, after everyone has gone back for many help-ings, and me for many refills, my teeth will be stained purple. I'll get up to go to the bathroom and, while zigzagging back to the table, I'll think, *As crazy as they are, I love these people.* I'll plop down in my chair and put my elbows on the table. "All I have to say," I'll slur, "is that we are *not* taking a goddamn Christmas card picture this year."

My mom, still in her monogrammed apron, will say, "For goodness sake, Lilibet, don't say that *word*. It's Christmas." She'll shake the ice in her fifth vodka-cran. "Now be a lady and fix your grandfather another drink."

Alone

■

I am a textbook Gemini, a true "twin," which basically just means I'm schizophrenic. While one part of me—Social Me—loves to be in the middle of the action, to make an entrance, to make people laugh, the other part of me—Solitary Me—practically breaks out in hives when my cell phone rings. I met a guy at a cocktail party, also a Gemini, and he summed it up better than I ever could. He said, "Either I am *running* the party or I am in a bathrobe, in the dark, watching Spanish television." (Never mind the fact that Peter and I are *both* Geminis, which is like four people in one relationship. On any given day, we're never quite sure which two people are going to show up.)

Writing speaks to this half-ness that consumes me so wholly. Writing feeds my need to connect and be alone at the same time. I want to write words that people will read, but in endeavoring to do so, I get the pure, uninterrupted luxury of being by myself. In the box, I get the best of both worlds, too: I am alone and not alone at the same time.

Smiling

■

I was wearing white shorts with pink flowers, a matching pink T-shirt, and a pair of Keds with no socks the first time I ran The Mile. My stringy blonde hair was not even pulled into a ponytail. I was in the fifth grade. This was back before we had to change clothes for gym class—that started in the sixth grade, around the same time we were told to start wearing deodorant. Running The Mile was part of the "Physical Fitness Challenge," a national standardized test. My elementary school didn't have a track, so a loop was constructed out of mini orange cones on the soccer field. Our gym teacher, Coach Caginello, was rotund around the midsection and always outfitted in a two-piece jogging suit that seemed to be sewn from the same material as the parachute we played with on rainy days. Coach's wind pants swished between his thighs when he walked—on the balls of his feet, always—and were tapered at the ankle by a band of ruched nylon. (In my memory, he only owned one jogging suit. It was teal and magenta, and he wore it every day.) Coach completed the look with a pair of high-top white Avivas, not dissimilar to those Zack Morris wore on *Saved by the Bell*, with a swipe of white Velcro where the tongue met the laces. On the day of The Mile run, Coach had an extra accessory: a stopwatch slung around his neck. We had to run ten laps to complete a mile, and we had to shout what lap we were on each time we passed go. Coach was keeping count, too.

I was the first girl to finish, and I beat almost all of the boys, too. I remember finishing and not being tired and wishing I had run faster and beaten everyone by even more. I remember the stunned look on Coach's face when I crossed the finish line. He must have told people at school because, over the next few days, teachers came up to me and said, "I hear you're quite the speed demon!"

It is amazing how powerful positive reinforcement can be to a child. From that physical fitness challenge forward, I thought of myself as someone who was good at running. And that belief, whether true or not, motivated me to run. In middle school, I took "running The Mile" in gym class embarrassingly seriously and relished seeing my name at the top of the list, year after year. As high school approached, I knew I'd play no other sports but cross-country and track. (This may have had to do with the fact that I was also awful at everything else.)

During high school, competitive running was a joy. I loved my teammates, my coaches; I loved the thrill of racing and of winning. I loved the freedom and independence that logging many miles alone along hilly, empty roads provided me. I even loved the excruciating track workouts. From that blinding, doubled-over pain came some of the greatest highs of my life.

By my junior year, I was All-County, All-State, All-New England, and on an All-American 4x800 meter relay team. By my senior year, I was also someone who would stand in front of the bathroom mirror, naked, and count her ribs for fun.

I idolized the skeleton-like elite women runners—the Olympians, the marathoners, the Kenyans—all sharp shoulders, shredded thighs, cut stomachs. Nothing but bone, skin, lean muscle, and tendon. So in addition to running many miles a week, I counted my calories meticulously. I would eat a half a piece of dry, whole-wheat toast before going on a ten-mile run. I wouldn't eat any fat. I wouldn't eat any carbs at dinner. I wouldn't even drink orange juice—my favorite drink as a kid—because I thought it was too caloric. Sometimes my stomach would wake me up in the middle of the night because it was so empty, and I would drink a glass of cold water to make the hunger go away. My hips narrowed, my chest was concave, my collarbone stuck out so far you could swing from it. Because I had so little body fat, I stopped menstruating. My doctor also told me I was suffering from bone loss—my bones were literally deteriorating because I had such a low body mass index. With college recruiting upon me, I went from being the tall, healthy homecoming queen I'd been crowned that fall to looking like an eleven-year-old boy.

People would tell me I was too skinny. The doctor told me I was too skinny. I would sit in her office, my hunched-over spine poking through the back of my hospital gown, and say, "Okay, I will eat more fat and carbs, I promise." Then I would leave and drink a bottle of water to stave off my starvation and smile. Every time someone told me I was too skinny, it just motivated me to stay that way. "Too skinny" wasn't an insult in my mind; it was a compliment. At track meets, I would push my tiny self so hard I often threw up right after my race— crossing the finish line and staggering half-conscious toward the nearest garbage can.

I was recruited to run for The University of Colorado, which was, and still is, one of the best Division I distance-running programs in the country. I wasn't an "official" recruit in that I didn't receive a scholarship to be on the team. I was a "walk-on." Based on my times in high school, I was someone they were interested in developing. An assistant coach called me a few times over the summer and told me how I should be training, how many miles I should be running. He said that when I got to Boulder at the end of August, I'd practice with the team, but in early September, I'd have to run a time trial to earn an actual spot on the roster.

Because I was just a walk-on, I started practicing with the team much later than everyone else. Most of them had arrived in early August to acclimate to the 5,300-foot elevation, and some had trained all summer in Boulder. Plus, in mid-August, they had all spent a weekend together at training camp, running and bonding at 7,000 feet. I missed all of that.

My second day in Boulder, I went to the field house to meet the head coach, Mark Wetmore, who is considered by many to be the best collegiate distance-running coach in the country. He was lean to the point of gaunt—hadn't missed a day of running in almost twenty years—and his hair was tied into a graying ponytail, tucked under a black Nike baseball hat. It was immediately apparent that he was a very serious guy. The screensaver on his office computer said, "Res severa verum gaudia," which he told me meant, "To be serious is the greatest joy." Wetmore was intimidating, but not unlikable. We chatted for a little while but he cut the conversation short, saying something like, "Well! Get out of here! Go run!" Wetmore was short on small talk. In his world, you did your talking with your feet. Two of the freshman girls on scholarship entered the office around that time. "Perfect!" he said, "They are headed out for a run, too."

The three of us trotted gingerly down a hill. *Wonderful,* I thought, *I can keep up with this pace.* Then we took a left on the Boulder Creek Path, and they started booking it. As their long, lean bodies bounded along like deer, they chatted easily about training camp and what they were doing for dinner that night. It was obvious that they were already friends. They tried to include me in the conversation, but the elevation rendered me incapable of talking. After two miles, I felt like I was choking on the thin mountain air, and I finally had to stop and walk. The girls didn't wait for me, which was fine. I knew I couldn't keep up. They took off ahead of me, just chatting away as if that pace, at that altitude, was nothing. There was a fork at the end of the creek path, and I was so far behind, I couldn't see which way they had turned. To the left was a narrow track ascending a steep hill. Seeing as these girls were clearly gluttons for pain, I figured this was the way we were supposed to go. Now, if altitude is a kick in the shins while running on flat ground, it is an absolute kick in the face while going up a hill. When I finally got to the top, I didn't see them. I was happy to be alone because, like a very tall and very skinny baby, I crumbled to the ground and started to cry.

Fortunately, acclimating to altitude is a real thing. By the following month I was able to summit that hill, and many much larger hills, without crying. I was also able to run fast enough in the time trial to make the team.

■

In high school, I was one of the leanest people on my team, but in college—training next to some of the best women in the world—I wasn't even close. Some of my teammates looked like they were going to die in their sleep. I heard a rumor that one girl, who was five foot ten, was not allowed to practice unless she weighed at least ninety pounds. *Ninety pounds*. Some of the girls on the team were covered in fuzzy yellow hair all over their arms, chests, and faces, and they were always complaining about being cold. I now know these are signs of anorexia. When we went out on training runs, we looked like a pack of skeletons, our size-extra-small spandex hanging loosely off our legs. The prevailing mentality was that every extra ounce on our bodies was extra weight we had to carry around the track. Thus, we wanted to have as little as possible. But with that came injuries, so at any given time, half our team was hurt, the other half winning NCAA championships.

At the end of the fall season, the top seven women on our team (I, of course, not being one of them) competed in the National Championships—and won. By that spring, I had bursitis and tendonitis in both my knees and stress fractures up and down my shins. From the sidelines, with ice packs taped to my legs, I'd watch these women wobble on toothpick-thin limbs. I was frustrated and disappointed, but more than anything, I was disheartened. This activity that had given me so much, that I had loved so much, I suddenly started to hate.

The following fall, I wrote a six-page handwritten letter to Coach Wetmore telling him I quit. I think I was writing it as much for myself as for him. I really struggled with the decision because I had loved running, more than anything. It had, in some ways, defined me as a human being. It gave me my role in the play. Conversations often went like this: "That's Lilibet; she's a runner. She probably ran, like, six miles today. Lilibet, how many miles did you run today?"

"Eight."

In the letter, I told him that running was no longer making me happy. That it was no longer fun. I told him I didn't feel like there was any sense of community on the team. These women were not supportive of one another; they were only competitive with each other. And you know what, they should have been. These were *literally* the best collegiate runners in the world. In individual sports like track and cross-country, your teammates are your competition.

In high school, my teammates were my sisters. We cried together when someone on the relay dropped the baton, held each other's hair back when someone barfed in the bathroom after a race. We yelled out each other's splits and yelled louder to get each other across the finish line. We stretched each other's hamstrings. That Pollyanna track team fantasy did not exist on the best Division I team in the country. At that level, it was all business. I wasn't going to find any hand-holding here. It was the 2004 Lakers, Kobe and Shaq on the same team. No one was passing the ball.

I bet I would have thrived on a Division II or Division III team. I would have probably been the captain. But at Colorado, I was struggling to keep up. Not to mention, I was missing college. Not classes, but everything else. For my teammates, running was everything. It was their identity. Their *entire* identity. This is not something to disparage. It takes an incredible amount of discipline and dedication and an excruciatingly high tolerance for pain. But for me, I knew running was just a part of my being, and in order to succeed at that sort of program, it had to be *every* part of you. My teammates would eat, sleep, and breathe running. I wasn't willing to do that.

Wetmore would often tell me I was one of the most inconsistent runners he'd ever coached. Some days, I was one of the first to finish a workout; other days I was pulling over to the side of the road, pretending to tie my shoes while heaving for breath and throwing up. During one particular twelve-mile-long run along Magnolia Road—a dirt road along a ridge at 8,000 feet, with a rolling, relentless ascent—I was struggling to put one foot in front of the other. Wetmore pulled up alongside me in one of the university-issued vans. "Late night at the sorority house?" he said, even though he knew I wasn't in a sorority. But still, he knew. He was on to me. He knew I was trying to play it both ways. To be the star runner and not miss the keg party.

In high school, I could get away with this. I had enough natural ability to pull it off. But in Division I athletics, everyone has natural ability. The difference was who decided to put in the work. For Wetmore, work ethic was everything. He expected a lot out of his runners, and in turn, he showed them the same level of diligence and commitment. Wetmore would give periodic speeches throughout the season. They weren't preachy or overwrought; they got the point across in the most straightforward way. (Not surprisingly, the one that sticks out most in my mind was given before winter break when he told us not to let ourselves go that next month, eating too many cookies and drinking too many beers.) In one of his more substantial speeches, which is recounted in the book *Running with the Buffaloes*, about the 1998 men's cross-country team, he said, "Look, this is what I am . . . I don't play golf. I don't have many hobbies. I don't have a wife. The bottom line is I'm here to make you guys run fast. When I go to sleep at night, my mind's churning, thinking of ways to make you go fast . . ."

At practice one afternoon, during a tempo run on the Creek Path, I had fallen well behind the pack and was stumbling along at a totally unrespectable pace. Wetmore—who often ran not with us, but behind us—passed me. As he did so, he had only one word for me. It was not yelled, but very calm, and very clear: "Work."

I think part of me was scared to give it my all. Wetmore was renowned in the collegiate community for turning more walk-ons into All-Americans than any other coach in NCAA history. I'm sure there was a part of me that feared this, that with enough success in this one realm, I'd have to sacrifice the rest of my life. What if I wanted to go skiing? Go to a concert? Eat a cupcake?

In my resignation letter, I didn't mention my concerns with what I considered to be rampant disordered eating on the team. Wetmore already knew about that. Eating disorders in women's distance running programs are so prevalent that a clinical diagnosis has even been assigned them: "The Female Athlete Triad," which is a condition that occurs when caloric intake does not match energy expenditure, causing disordered eating, menstrual dysfunction, and premature osteoporosis.

This is present, to some degree, in all collegiate track programs, but it was notorious at Colorado. (My senior year, I interviewed Wetmore for the student newspaper, and he admitted they towed a fine line. That you had to. It was a dangerous but necessary line, with the highest level of fitness on one side and injuries on the other.) *Why should I say something in the letter?* I reasoned. I knew it wasn't going to change. And it never will. Look at all the Olympians and the people winning the big-ticket marathons: They are whittled to the bone.

When I walked away from the team the fall of my sophomore year, I walked away from running for a long time. I started to eat normally again. Without the internal and external pressures to be so thin, I was able to enjoy food like I used to. I ate the cheeseburger, the fries, *and* the milkshake. (There was a time, during the height of my running "career," when I could not remember the last time I had eaten ice cream. Also during this time, I remember beating myself up for days after a barbeque because I had chosen the burger over the grilled chicken.) No longer consumed by a constant quest for perfection, I got back to a healthy weight. Flesh returned to my arms. My stringy thighs once again filled out my jeans. My butt was no longer just a muscle. The bony column down the center of my sternum gradually transitioned from a cage that protected my lungs and heart to a chest—a woman's chest. I finally looked less like an eleven-year-old boy and more like a woman.

A couple of years later, while watching several of my former teammates compete in the Olympic Trials (two of them would go on to compete in the 2008 Olympics in Beijing), it was impossible not to wonder, with an almost unbearable sense of regret, what if I had stayed with it? I was reminded of my cousin Marian's high school valedictorian speech in 1993. I was eleven at the time, a very impressionable age for a girl. In her speech, Marian quoted John Greenleaf Whittier: "Of all sad words of tongue or pen, the saddest are these, 'it might have been.'" I immediately scribbled it into my diary. I am not blaming this on Marian, but all my life I have lived under this sort of fear of unrealized potential, constantly tallying the what-ifs. Why was I given this gift of being good at something if I wasn't going to take it to the point of self-actualization? What if I had given it my full effort? Could I, too, be at the Olympics? It was depressing to think about.

I became obsessed with the careers of my old teammates. Most of them were still running competitively, many were sponsored. I looked up their results at meets, watched their races on YouTube, followed them on Twitter. I Googled pictures of them mid-stride at races: still skinny, still fit, now really into compression socks. In a decidedly masochistic move, I even dug out my old University of Colorado racing buns—the tight bottoms we wore to meets, which looked like a pair of shiny, full-bottomed underpants—and tried them on. Between the Olympic Trials, the Internet-stalking, and the sight of my butt coming out of those buns in directions I did not know were possible, it was clear that I needed to start running again.

The fact was, I missed it. I felt like a very important piece of my identity was gone. A guy I had been hanging out with for a fairly long time said to me one day, "Wait, you run?" Not even, "Wait, you're a *runner*?" He didn't even know that I occasionally went for a jog. The truth is, at that point in my life, I wasn't someone who occasionally went for a jog. I *felt* like a runner, though. In an abstract and semi-deluded way, I still thought of myself as a runner. For this reason, I wasn't willing to give up on that part of my identity entirely.

When I decided to start running again, I approached it from a much healthier place, both mentally and physically. This time, it was a hobby and not a sport. I was no longer a runner who was trying to prove anything, who was trying to be the best at anything. I ran for myself only. With this newfound freedom, I remembered why I loved to run. Running was my yoga. And believe me, as someone who has been known to, perhaps, heckle yoga a bit (too many years waiting on mat-wielding yogis who only ordered green tea), it is hard for me to say that without sounding sarcastic. Be assured: I am not being sarcastic. There is something incredibly meditative about listening to myself breathe, feeling my feet strike the ground—*clip, clip, clip, clip*—while tasting the sweat drip off my nose, salt slipping into my mouth.

Before I knew it, running was once again a daily ritual, a commune with myself, the air, the ocean. I'd run along the beachfront boardwalk most days—standstill traffic to my right, the moody and mesmeric Pacific to my left. For the most part, I would head north from Venice, leaving the bums, the barkers, and the fire-blowers behind, seeking something less chaotic. Along the boardwalk, there is a dramatic shift in scenery where Venice meets Santa Monica. The drum circles, dread-locks, and pop-up shops peddling plastic neon sunglasses and T-shirts that say "Yes We Cannabis" give way to outdoor yoga classes, moms pushing strollers, and white high-rise apartment complexes with names like "The Sands" and "Sea Colony." It's less heroin-addicts-on-the-run, more middle-aged-dads-out-for-a-run. In Santa Monica, I'd twist through the tourists on rented banana-seat beach cruisers and slip under the Santa Monica Pier, where I was always sure I would be stabbed. It was a dark, dank stretch under that pier, a mammoth structure at the end of Colorado Boulevard, which operated as a year-round mini amusement park, complete with a Ferris wheel, clowns, and cotton candy, all hurtling into the Pacific. A cor-nucopia of carnival noises would echo above me while I ran through that corridor: the synthesized fairytale tones of the merry-go-round, the *clickity-clack-clack* of a loop-less roller coaster, the sounds of accordions and organs clashing in their own discordant warble, and children shrieking every human emotion on the spectrum.

On the other side—fortunately, I never got stabbed—peace. The boardwalk was empty, serene, salubrious. I'd normally only make it as far north as Pacific Palisades (or, on more ambitious runs, Malibu), where there was nothing but the occasional cyclist, surfers, and me. I'd smell the ocean (while I am not particularly fond of getting in the cold Pacific, I love its musky sulfur smell), and I'd watch the surfers: slick, black, human-sized seals bobbing up and over the waves. I'd breathe. Running was no longer about pain or a pursuit of perfection. At last, it was a pleasure again.

On Christmas Eve, about a year after I returned to running, I was at a party with one of my longtime friends, Jan, who was also one of my former high school track teammates. We were standing around the dining room table when she suggested we run a marathon. I thought she had had too much eggnog. Her sister Beth jumped in, too. "No really, I think we should. I've been looking at the marathon schedules." They had been planning this. They knew, plied with enough bourbon and cured ham, I was bound to agree to anything.

"Eh, I don't think that's such a great idea," I said.

Two hours later, with the help of eggnog, gingerbread, and grappa-soaked cherries, my Christmas carol changed its tune.

"You know what," I said, leaning against a wall to stretch my calves/hold myself up, "A marathon sounds like a great idea!"

By the time I piled in the backseat of my parents car (because even as an adult child, I still ride in the backseat), we had picked our race: The Portland Marathon in early October. That gave us plenty of time to train, and we'd always wanted to go to Portland anyway.

Jan and Beth both ran collegiate track as well: Jan for four years at Duke, and Beth for a year or so at George Washington. They both continued running after college. Not competitively, but almost daily, Jan especially. They shared an apartment in San Francisco, so they'd be able to train together and keep each other on a strict regimen. Unlike Jan and Beth, I put off training until the absolute last minute. While most people train for a marathon for four months or more, I waited until there were only five weeks to go. I downloaded a famous marathoner's six-week training schedule (tagline: "There's Still Time!") and chopped off the first week. I was working freelance from home, so I had plenty of time to get in my mileage. And while I love running alone, the long runs got, well, long. I listened to music on my iPod, to books on tape, to any distraction from the oppressive understanding that, while I was one hour into a run, I still had another hour to go. Plus, I was training in September, one of LA's hottest months. For my twenty-mile run two weeks before the marathon, I had a friend drop me off at a shopping center in Palos Verdes, which is still in LA County, but barely. I ran from there, along the boardwalk, all the way to Malibu, where my run ended with me sitting on the floor of a gas station, slumped against the refrigerator, drinking thirty-two ounces of green Gatorade without stopping for a breath. I think I sufficiently freaked out the gas station attendant, who thought I was having a heat stroke. He gave me an icepack for my forehead and called a cab to get me home. I think it's fair to say, after that twenty-miler, I was feeling many miles from "ready."

The night before the Portland marathon, we set out for dinner before sunset, along with several dozen other people dining in running shoes. We ate pasta with Jan and Beth's parents and Jan's boyfriend, who had all flown to Portland to watch the race. (I told my parents not to come since I was certain I was going to embarrass myself, or die. It just wasn't worth the trip.) Earlier that day we stopped by the race expo to pick up our bib numbers and the little chips for our shoes. Jan's dad had picked up some wristbands, which broke down the mile-splits for various finishing times, and was handing them out at dinner while talking about our race strategies.

(In attendance at every single high school track meet with a stopwatch around his neck, he was a sort of honorary coach. My dad, on the other hand, would read the newspaper in a far corner of the field house, emerging only to yell, "Go Pork-chop!" as I rounded a turn mid-race.) Jan's dad leaned over her plate of spaghetti and pointed excitedly at one of the wrist-bands. Jan had set a fairly lofty goal for herself—to run faster than 3:40 and qualify for The Boston Marathon—and he was walking her through her target mile times: 8:23 for the first mile, 16:47 through two, under one hour fifty minutes at the halfway point. Beth was less intense but still wanted to do well, examining a pace bracelet for the four-hour finishing group. I pointed at the wristband outlining a ten-minute-per-mile marathon pace and joked that I'd probably finish somewhere around there. I refused to wear a bracelet, though, because I was too scared that I might have to run even slower than that.

The next morning we woke before sunrise. We ate bananas and untoasted bagels with peanut butter and honey, and pulled our hair into ponytails. We sipped Gatorade and stretched our quads, crammed into a corner between a hotel room bed and a fake mahogany dresser. I insisted we play "Eye Of The Tiger" on my iPod speakers to get pumped up. (Did I think we were going to box the Russians?) Actually (and perhaps more embar-rassingly) it was in honor of our high school's mascot, a tiger.

An hour later, we were dropped off near the starting line. In the still-dark chill of an early October Oregon morning, we waded through the crowds, wearing spandex and tank tops, and over that, warmer layers we were willing to strip off on the course and lose forever. Around my waist, a small zippered pouch, which can only be accurately described as a "fanny pack," was holstered above my hips by a belt of nylon web-bing. I had stocked it with five packets of energy gel and five Advil—a customer at Chaya had told me to take one of each every hour. (The night before I left for Portland I realized I had asked no one for any advice on how to actually run a marathon. A man eating a basket of fried calamari at table 63—who said he'd run three—seemed like an expert-enough opinion.) My ponytail was pulled through the back of a hat I'd bought a few days before at a running store on Washington Boulevard in Venice—lightweight and ventilated and not something I would ever wear under ordinary circumstances. But these were not ordinary circumstances. I was about to run twenty-six miles, *in a row*. As we passed more and more runners who looked like my former collegiate teammates— the high and hollow cheekbones, the quads so defined you could see every tendon, the biceps that always looked flexed, even when their hands were hanging loosely at mid-thigh—I began to think, *What am I doing?* I had signed myself up for a lot of dumb things in my twenties, but this might well be the dumbest, I thought. I had barely trained and, during my twenty-mile run—the most important, and telling, of all marathon training—I had nearly died.

As the start of the race neared, it was not dark, but not yet light. The temperature was in the low-60s, and it was spitting rain. We sipped water, but not too much—another tip from my calamari-eating Sherpa—and shook out our legs. We ran a few ten- or twenty-yard strides—as far as we could go without running into a person or a fence—and stretched in a semi-circle. Jan jumped up and down in place, like a frog, her heels hitting her in the butt, something she used to do on the starting line at track meets. Her parents had flown across the country from Connecticut, and her brand-new boyfriend was watching, too. Jan was short on words before the marathon, tense and focused—shaking out her arms, rolling her neck, like I'd seen her do at so many meets before.

I think seeing the pressure she was putting on herself actually calmed me down. There was, after all, no pressure on me. I wasn't attempting to hit a target time; I wasn't trying to qualify for anything. I was not *racing* this marathon; I was just *running* it. *Jogging* it. Perhaps even *walking* it. Unlike my former teammates at Colorado, I was not running twenty-six miles at a five-minute pace to win—or even, like Jan, twenty-six miles at an eight-minute pace to qualify for a more important race. I was, instead, running it like a middle-aged math teacher from Long Beach: just to see if I could finish. With that in mind, I began to relax. *I have nothing to lose,* I thought. Though I was surrounded by thousands of people in every direction—race participants, spectators, volunteers—I was comforted by this thought: No one was watching me. No one was even waiting to hear my finishing time back in LA. I had barely told anyone I was running a marathon. No one—here, there, or elsewhere— had any expectations for me. *I* had no expectations for me. There was no one to let down, including myself.

With that, I embraced the pre-race frenzy with a sort of agnostic abandon. *Who cares how well I do? Who cares how quickly, or slowly, I finish the thing?* I mean, keeling over dead would be sort of a bummer, but, with no pressure to go fast, I could simply forestall that from happening by stopping to walk. A couple of minutes before the gun was fired, we joined the masses of people packed for blocks behind the starting line. With my finger readied on the start button of my rubber Timex watch, I reminded Jan and Beth for the fiftieth time, "Do not wait for me. Go without me." Then I wished them luck and slapped them both firmly on the ass.

When the starting gun fired, Jan and Beth took off at a quick clip and disappeared into a sea of runners darting down the street. (We were many blocks behind the "real" start, where the elite runners take off at a pace faster than the maximum speed for most treadmills.) With my fanny pack shifted to my fanny, I set out at a slow trot. I was running, but not much faster than the average person ambles. I am certain I could have speed-walked faster. At nine minutes, fifty-eight seconds,

I looked down at my watch and let out a nervous laugh: I hadn't even run a mile. And I had *twenty-five* more to go after that. I began to panic.

The farthest I had ever raced was a half-marathon, and immediately upon crossing the finish, I beelined for the medic tent, dehydrated and delirious. *My god,* I thought, *how dehydrated and delirious will I be after running twice that distance? How will I not hurt myself, pass out, crumble to the ground and die?* I worried, forcing one foot in front of the other. People were passing me by the dozens. Men and women both—some younger than me, many older than my parents—surged past, leaving me to look at their fanny packs. Like being engulfed by a wave and sucked farther out to sea, the packs of people overtaking me made me feel like I was going backward, not forward. *How is everyone running so fast?* I thought. *That man is at least seventy-five; who is he to come out of the gates so hot? Do these people not know how long this thing is?* I wondered. Though it pained me to admit, I knew the truth: These people had trained properly. They could easily maintain that pace for twenty-six miles. Unlike me, they were prepared.

I began berating myself, angry that I put myself in this position. *Why hadn't I trained better?* I had no excuse, after all. I had more than enough time, yet I had waited until the last minute. When I finally started to train, I gave it far from my full effort. I didn't even take it seriously. Now I was only a few miles into the race, and I was totally panicked about the task ahead.

Jan and Beth's parents were standing at Mile 3 and Mile 10. Somehow they didn't see me at either stop. "I thought we should call the hospitals," their mom said after the race. Their dad said, "Nah, I told her, if anything, you were at the bar." At Mile 3, I would have agreed that either were plausible options: Before I got to that finish line, I was bound to either collapse or quit.

But somehow, by Mile 10, I was still clicking along. I did not feel like I was going to fall over; I did not want to seek shelter in a nearby bar. Along the route, hundreds of locals lined the streets, cheering on the race participants. Bands played, gospel choirs sang, cars honked their horns, children handed out orange slices on their front lawns. Strangers rang cowbells and shouted words of encouragement. "You can do it! You're doing great!" they'd say, a child perched on top of their shoulders, holding a hand-painted poster for Mom. The scene was incredibly moving. I felt like the whole city was giving me a high-five.

Perhaps I got swept up in the momentum of all the roadside support, but mile after mile, I began increasing my speed. I went from running something slower than a ten-minute mile, to nine and a half minutes per mile to something faster than a nine-minute mile. A friend had told me, "At Mile 13 you'll feel great, and by Mile 18 you'll want to curl up in a ball and cry." (This was a grown man.) As I approached the half-marathon mark—the distance that had at one time rendered me in need of an IV—I was shocked to realize that he was right: at Mile 13, I did feel great. Not fine. Not okay. *Great.*

Twenty-six miles is a long time to reflect on what exactly it is you are doing. Living in Venice, in one of the few walkable communities in LA, I rarely even *drive* twenty-six miles. *There is something pretty remarkable about the fact that the only equipment I am using to travel this distance is a pair of shoes and my body,* I thought. My legs, my lungs, that's it. I started to hit a plateau of sorts, where my legs were turning over comfortably and confidently. To use a running cliché, I hit my stride.

At Mile 16, there was a huge hill, the incline of which stretched for almost three-quarters of a mile. People were peeling over to the side, walking, some stopping to throw up. I pumped my arms and popped up the hill on the balls of my feet, focusing on the ground in front of me. Somehow, while summiting that hill, I *still* felt great. *How is this even possible?* I thought. *Maybe it's the mini Dixie Cups of Gatorade I've been drinking along the way? Maybe it's the Goo packets? The Advil?* I was at a loss. In what was most certainly a risky move, I decided to speed up on the hill. Save for when I blew by a row of Porta Potties, it was the first time I passed anyone. I picked off one person, then two, then many.

Well that was fun, I thought as I whizzed past a pack of people. *Suckers.* All of a sudden, I was channeling that inner child who loved beating the Bugle Boys off the kids in my fifth-grade class. In the most unlikely of places, somewhere around mile seventeen, I was remembering what it was that I loved about running in the first place: It was fun. As children, we ran because it was our favorite way to get from one place to the other. It was instinctive, automatic. Have you ever seen a child walk toward a playground? Maybe if he was holding an ice cream cone. *Maybe.* As a kid, running was a reward, something we got to do when we busted out of the confines of our schools, or our homes. (Unfortunately, I think that fun gets hammered out of it around age ten when team sports become more competitive and running is turned into a form of punishment. "If you're late for practice, you have to run five laps," coaches would bark.) By channeling my Keds-wearing, sockless, fifth-grade self, I enjoyed running the marathon. *This is a race,* I thought. A race is meant to be fun. When children race, whether it's while hopping in a potato sack or with their ankles tied together, it is something to look forward to.

Plus, passing those people felt *good.* Suddenly the competitive spirit I had suppressed for so many years was finding its way to the surface. Who was I kidding? Of course I cared how I did. Of course I wanted to do well. I was *not* just the math teacher from Long Beach doing a marathon just to see if he could finish. I *was* a real runner, damnit.

After the hill, the St. Johns Bridge crossed the Willamette River for most of Mile 17. A bunch of red balloons bobbed in the air forty yards in front of me, tied to the back of a pace-setter. He was surrounded by a large pack of runners trying to stay on target for a four-hour finishing time. *I can't believe I caught the four-hour group,* I thought. *For the first several miles, I was moving about as fast as a toddler crawls. Actually, I think toddlers are faster.* Because I knew there was no way I could complete a marathon in less than four hours, I settled in behind the group and steadied my pace. *Just keep it right here; follow them for the duration,* I thought. But those stupid red balloons were taunting me: "Betcha can't catch me." *Oh, I betcha I can.* I sped up again, passing the four-hour pace group, and everyone else on the bridge.

I know this sounds deranged—I must have been *really* de-hydrated and totally delirious, like a lost backpacker in Death Valley who hallucinates a river, but in addition to being very hydrated, I felt absolutely, euphorically, amazing. So amazing that the marathon felt *easy.* Too easy. Again I berated myself. *Maybe I am actually good at running marathons,* I thought. *Why had I so underestimated myself?*

Racing through Mile 18, I was overcome by the realization that I had barely trained, and yet, running a marathon felt easy. I was angry at this half-heartedness that had followed me through my life, that had plagued my college career. I thought back to my cousin's valedictorian speech, bemoaning the "what might have beens." *Why didn't I train harder? Maybe I could have been competitive? Maybe I could have qualified for Boston? Why do I always do this? Why do I give up before I know where I could really go with something? Maybe I shouldn't have quit the team? Maybe, who knows, maybe I could have been an elite marathoner, like so many of my former teammates? What if? What if? Goddamnit what if?*

I grabbed a cup of water off a table at Mile 19, took a small sip, and tossed the cup behind me. *I wonder if my brother ever tallies the what-ifs,* I thought, steadying into my stride. He was something of a golf prodigy as a child, winning tournaments all over the country. He went on to play for the University of North Carolina, where he had a mediocre collegiate career. Now he watches as many of the guys he used to beat as a junior—Trevor Immelman, Bubba Watson, Lucas Glover—win The Masters and the U.S. Open. I am sure he must sometimes wonder *what if.* What if he had trained harder in college? What if he had given it his all? Could he, too, be winning major tournaments? *I should ask him about this next week,* I thought. But I never did. I knew he'd just give me some sarcastic response. That's another thing he and I have in common: We use humor as a defense mechanism.

I targeted the next pack of people in front of me. The what-ifs weren't relevant now. Beating myself up over my lack of training wasn't going to do any good at this point. There was nothing left to do but run as fast as I could. As I passed the twenty-mile marker, I focused on how many people I could pass in six miles.

I focused on lengthening my stride, using the reserves I had leftover from my very conservative start. I quickened my pace and continued to pass people—as many as I could catch—for the rest of the race. Someone from the sideline yelled, "Great pace, green!"—I was wearing green—"Way to finish strong!" I wanted to yell back, "You know what, I feel fucking strong!" He was flanked by children, though, so I gave him a double thumbs-up instead.

Even if it was from a stranger, I enjoyed this acknowledgement. As it turned out, I liked knowing that someone was watching. *Why hadn't I told more people I was running the marathon? Why hadn't I made my parents come watch?* But I knew why: In the event I failed, there'd be no one there to witness. I had fooled everyone—even myself—into believing I wasn't going to try. That I didn't really care. But somewhere along that twenty-six-mile journey I realized: I did care. Of course I cared. I will always care.

With less than a mile to go, I pumped my arms and got up on my toes, which, in runner speak, means I ran really fast. I rounded the last corner, where there was actually a fat lady singing—nice touch, Portland—and blew through the final stretch like it was my own personal Olympics. On the other side of the finish line, race participants were in various forms of crumpled. Those still standing walked like they were drunk. I know I sound like a mental person, but I could have kept running. It was just like that day in fifth grade, when I wished I had run faster and beaten everyone by even more.

There's a framed picture of me running across the bridge during the marathon, and people will look at it and say, "Are you smiling? You're such a dork, I can't believe you smiled when you saw the cameraman." But I didn't see the cameraman. I was just smiling.[10]

---

10 In an ironic twist, in June of 2012, I was on the cover of *Runner's World*. Not as a runner, but as a "fitness model."

I Love You!

■

A very drunk man with a very thick accent somehow wiggles himself behind the concierge desk, trips toward the box, and bangs on the glass with both fists, bellowing, "I love youuuuuuuu!"

The concierge grabs him gently by the bicep and says, "Sir, she cannot interact with the hotel guests. Please move away from the box." I can't help but feel sorry for the guy. The man steps back and almost falls over, then stumbles, one leg crossing in front of the other, toward the elevators.

Diorama

I just tossed my head back, slapped my thigh (which is bare, so it hurt), and let loose a wild deluge of laughter, swishing blonde strands across my back. I'm on the phone with Heather, and she's pretty funny, but not *that* funny. Lately, I've been catching myself indulging in such theatrics while I'm in the box.

Fearing that the artificiality of this whole situation has rendered me something less than human, I find myself over-acting. *See, people, I am real!* When I'm reading something that's funny, I laugh hard. Much harder than I would in my *real* living room. And that night when I cried in the box, I have to wonder: Did I enjoy it? Just a little? I think I did. *Over here, people, see? I cry real tears! Look at them! They're wet! And my snot is snotty! I am not just a cardboard cutout in a diorama!* The false reality of this set has made me hyper-real—an exaggeratedly human version of myself who relies on explosive guffaws and dramatic, arms-stretched-high-above-the-head yawns.

Bathroom Choreography

I shouldn't have brought this bottle of water into the box with me tonight. I'm not even halfway through the shift, and I already need to go to the bathroom. Here goes nothing.

In order to get out of the box to go to the bathroom, I have to pull off the following tricky and somewhat humiliating maneuvers:

1. Crawl across the box on my hands and knees.
2. Push open the door with a rather forceful shove.
3. Hang the top half of my body off the end of the mattress.
4. While hanging upside down, reach below the mattress and retrieve the stepladder.
5. Open the stepladder and place it next to the box, still hanging upside down.
6. Fling my legs out from under me so I am facing forward in a sitting position, my legs dangling below.
7. Step down the ladder while steadying myself with the handrails.

8. Collapse the ladder and put it back into the storage space.
9. Retrieve my jeans, shoes, and sweater or sweatshirt from my bag, which are stored next to the ladder.
10. Dress myself in these items, pulling them over my uniform while standing next to the empty box.

I have noticed this process attracts some attention. Because it is something of a production, yes, but also because the people in the lobby can't believe this perplexing creature is allowed out at her own free will. (Or that she stays in at her own free will.) And that she wears regular human clothes. It will be during one of these transitions that I'll see a group of guys elbowing each other, saying something like, "Dude, dude, check this out," while pointing a beer bottle in my direction.

I've decided it's the same sort of fascination and horror fourth graders have when they run into their teacher in the grocery store parking lot. *Whoa, whoa, whoa, Mrs. Belote has kids? She drives a car? She shops at the same supermarket as us? She's . . . she's . . . real?* I know I felt that way. I guess I always assumed all the teachers at Farmingville Elementary School slept under their desks. It never occurred to me that they paraded about in the real world, buying iceberg lettuce and wearing the same tennis shoes as my mom. It's unsettling to see something outside the only context you know. I hate to burst the hotel guests' weird art installation fantasies, but I do not live in here. This is not my only outfit. I use the bathroom just like you! I can climb up and down ladders! I ate a Crunch Wrap Supreme from Taco Bell on my way to work!

Outside the Box

■

There's a standup comedian in the lobby bar tonight. It's hard for me to hear him. It's also hard not to wonder if he's telling jokes about me. I'm such an easy target in here. I eventually give up trying to listen and put in my headphones.

A few minutes later, I get up to go to the bathroom. As I wheel around the corner, I almost trip over the people in line. This is a first. There is a line. Normally I can just zoom in and out; I'm back in the box before anyone notices.

"Oh," I say, and take my place in line, self-conscious of the fact that wearing jeans over my white shorts makes it look like I'm wearing a diaper.

A man, fiftyish, standing in front of me asks, "How are you tonight?"

"I'm good," I say. "I mean, I'm in the box."

He must have thought this was a figure of speech like, "I'm in the zone."

"Are you enjoying the comedian?" he asks.

"Well, I can't really hear him," I say, shaking my head.

The man nods in agreement.

"He's not projecting his voice very well. You must be sitting in the back like me."

"Yeah," I say and nod politely, not sure what to do with my hands with no drink, no purse, and no phone to fiddle with.

A minute later a thirty-something guy with shoulder-length hair gets in line behind me. He points at me, then at the empty box, then back at me.

"No . . ." he says. "You're the girl in the box?"

"Yep, it's true, they let us out to go to the bathroom."

"No way."

"Yes way."

"How long are you in there for?"

"Four hours," I say. "It used to be seven."

"Yeah, I remember coming in a couple years ago, and you guys were in there forever."

I smile, half-laugh, and go into the bathroom. When I come out, he's still there, leaning against the wall, thumbing his iPhone. He stops me as I walk past.

"Hey, sorry," he says. "I'm just so curious."

"It's fine, a lot of people are."

"So you can do whatever in there?" He seems genuinely bewildered.

"Yeah, there's Wi-Fi and everything," I say, tapping my fingers over an imaginary keyboard.

"And you can talk on the phone?" he asks.

"Yep. There really aren't any rules. We can even sleep."

A hotel employee walks by, so I start inching back toward the box. "Sorry, but we're not supposed to 'fraternize' with guests." I put air quotes around "fraternize."

"Well, I'm not a guest," he says. "I'm a guest of a guest. I have a real home. I mean, I have a home. I mean, I don't live here. I mean, I'm not a guest of the hotel."

He lets out an embarrassed laugh and asks, "Would you like to get a coffee sometime?"

"I'd love to (I lie) but—"

"Let me guess: boyfriend."

"Yes."

"Ah, right," he says. "I had to try. You just look so good in that box."

Amsterdam

I'm in the box sifting through old emails, the ones collecting dust at the bottom of the inbox, clicking "unsubscribe" whenever I can. I'm on an unsubscribe spree—J.Crew, MoveOn, Rent The Runway, Alzheimer's Association, Goodreads, Victoria's Secret. I scroll to the bottom, find UNSUBSCRIBE, which is usually in caps but always buried at the very end, click it, enter my email address, breathe. Wait, maybe I don't want to unsubscribe from J.Crew. They do have great sales . . . but they send three emails a day.

This is what I'm doing when I hear the words that shattered my sense of separation and safety. Standing at the front desk, a man with an indistinguishable accent eyes me and curls a thick finger at the concierge to signal, "Come here." He leans across the desk and asks, conspiratorially, "Is she for sale?"

My eyes dart down at the man. His eyes are fixed on me.

The concierge replies, "Oh, no, sir. No, no. She's just part of the installation."

I stare at my computer screen, but my eyes won't focus on anything. I feel totally naked. Does this man believe he can rent me by the hour? Take me up to his hotel room and have his way with me?

Does he think this is like the Red Light District in Amsterdam? I went there while studying abroad in London, and I remember those streets and those windows—the rows and rows of ladies in waiting. For some reason, I remember one girl more than the others. Maybe because she was so young. She was wearing a nightgown and sitting on a stool in front of a vanity, combing her hair, waiting for a paying customer to pick her out like a puppy at a pet store. Probably not wanting to be picked out at all. That image and a single thought are burned into my memory: *How did this beautiful young girl end up here?* And now I can't help but wonder: *Are people thinking the same about me?*

All my nights in the box, I have never felt degraded. I've never seen it as something sexual or demeaning. I think of myself as part of an interesting experiment. But that man's voice—so authoritative, so demanding—won't get out of my head.

Is she for sale?

Gobble, Gobble

Sometimes the art installations in the box are seasonal. One January, the word "Resolve" hung from the front window, glowing in purple neon. The back wall was covered in New Year's resolutions, which were scribbled in sidewalk chalk: Call your mom. Floss. Take a lover.

Tonight, it seems the box artist has a real passion for Thanksgiving. Or maybe just a sick sense of humor. He's covered the back wall with a blown-up photograph of an overweight man wearing a tie and a Rolex, the sleeves of his white oxford cloth shirt rolled up over his fat, furry forearms. The man has a knife in one hand and a fork in the other. He is clearly preparing to carve a turkey, except there is no turkey. There is just me. So I guess he is preparing to carve me. On the front pane of glass, it says, "Gobble, Gobble," and all around me are papier-mâché carrots, gourds, pumpkins, and squash.

Things Even I Am Unwilling to Do

Box Girls—[11]

I need a show of hands who is available and willing to work on NYE.

The shift is from 7PM–2AM and pays $200.

You will be provided with a gold bikini and will be painted all gold . . .[12]

The theme of the night is "Gold '09"

You will be wearing a gold bathing suit and will be hanging out by the pool . . . swimming . . . hanging out . . .[13] Bathing suits and robes will be provided, as will a special table for all three of you, drinks, along with a heating lamp. I'm pretty sure it will be OK to invite a friend to come along and

---

11 An actual email from management.

12 Oh, like how that secretary was murdered in *Goldfinger*.

13 You already said "hanging out."

hang out at the table, but I will double-check . . . The pool
will be heated and no guests will be allowed in the pool. It's
just for the three of you to use and look pretty in.[14] :)

If you are interested, could you please forward me a recent
photo of yourself along with your measurements . . . and
don't forget to include your height and weight![15]

---

14 I'm thinking that wet and cold and painted all gold we wont look so
much "pretty" as "freakish." But thanks for the smiley face, it's somewhat
reassuring.

15 No.

Clare

I couldn't get the man's words out of my head. "Is she for sale?" I decided to talk to Clare about this, because not only had Clare been a Box Girl, but she went on to work for The Standard in the design department.

We met at a party hosted by *Flaunt*. It was at a new clothing boutique on Melrose Avenue and was sponsored by a vodka company, so the signature drink, complete with floating cranberries, was free. Clare and I stood in the corner by the bar and rested our free drinks on top of a garbage can.

We looked around the room while we talked. There were lots of guys with beards and long hair—"Stillwaters," I used to call them, because they look like they could be in that band from *Almost Famous*. I went through a stage in my single days when I loved Stillwater-types. Now my husband, Peter—tall, blonde, all-American boy—looks nothing like the Stillwaters. I sometimes find myself watching these men, wondering what they would look like without the hair, the mustache, the beard, the mask? Would they still look "cool?" Would they still *be* "cool?" How much of their identity is tangled up in all that hair?

Clare and I decided to take a lap. We saw Luis, still the editor of *Flaunt,* holding court on the sidewalk outside of the shop. His arms were flailing and his philosophizing was rapid and unrelenting—*how we've got to help each other out, how that's what it's all about, how in this business, in this economy, we've got to look out for each other, you know what I mean?*

We saw the old assistant to the publisher, who speaks with that flirty Hispanic inflection, that quick, quick, quick clip and then the slow, burning finish—the last word dragged out and flipped up at the end, as if everything is said with a touch of attitude.

We saw a former intern at *Flaunt*, who was also a model, and wanted you to know it, but was also quick to amend that admission with, "And I went to Berkeley."

When Clare and I returned to our corner by the garbage can, I was finally able to ask her about the box.

She immediately launched into hotel design–speak.

"You go to a hotel and you can be whoever you want to be," she said. "So people walk into The Standard, and the first thing they see is this girl, doing whatever she wants to do, being whoever she wants to be."

From the neck up—Nordic-blonde, blue eyes, Popsicle pink lips even without lipstick—Clare looks like she should be a greeter at a J.Crew in Greenwich, Connecticut. But from the shoulders down, she is covered in tattoos.

"Okay," I said. "But why do they have to be girls?"

Then came art school–speak.

"You have to remember the origin of art is the woman's body. That was one of the first forms of art."

I let out a slow and unconvinced, "Okay," stabbing a cranberry with my straw.

"I'm of the school where something like this is celebrating the woman's body, not degrading it. All the girls are dressed the same but they are all different shapes and sizes."

"Really?"

"Yes. They're not all model-looking girls. Not at all."

"Huh," I said, nodding my head.

I did not know that. I had always assumed, based on nothing more than email correspondence, that they were, in fact, model-type girls. I had received countless emails asking me to cover shifts for girls who had castings, or callbacks, or, for one obligation I will never forget, because a Box Girl was "recovering from breast augmentation."

I share this with Clare.

"Some are. But not all. That's not the point. It's supposed to be a peek into human nature, not just a display case for guys to look at pretty girls."

I replied, "Well that's what I had always thought, had always hoped, until I heard a man ask if I was for sale."

She already knows this story.

"That was one time," she said briskly. "So the girls are all in the same outfit, but each one of them is different, and they are all doing different things. Some read, some sleep, some play guitar. You write, for instance."

Driving home that night I thought about this. I thought about how, for the most part, I agreed with Clare. I tried to figure out why. Why was I okay with sitting in a box wearing so little clothing?

Panopticon

An older lady in a black button-down blouse and thick, tortoiseshell glasses is resting an elbow on the front desk, staring. No, *glaring*. I peek at her quickly and shrink back to my book. I now understand what it means to "steal glances" or look at something "out of the corner of your eye." Since the most important Box Girl rule is "no eye contact," I have to be sneaky about it—observing slyly, peripherally. I'm not supposed to make eye *contact*, but they say nothing about *looking*. With this woman, though, I don't need to look. Judgmental eyes, after all, are meant to be felt, not seen.

Some nights, if the lights in the box are particularly bright, I can't see anything. The glass becomes reflective, and I'm in bondage to the gaze of others. It's like being alone in a house at night with wall-to-wall windows and no blinds. On nights like this, the box becomes a sort of Panopticon—the circular-style prisons conceived in the late eighteenth century by English philosopher Jeremy Bentham. With a surveillance station in the middle and cells facing toward the center, a guard could observe the inmates without them knowing whether or not they were being observed. Central to Bentham's design was the idea that, not only were the guards able to view the prisoners at all times, but also, and most importantly, that the prisoners could not see the guards, thus ever-unsure whether they were under surveillance. Bentham described the Panopticon as "a new mode of obtaining power of mind over mind" and "a mill for grinding rogues honest."

The French philosopher Michel Foucault was fascinated by Bentham's design and argued that the Panopticon scenario forced prisoners to govern their own behavior, assuming they cared about the repercussions of bad behavior. Foucault believed prisoners would regulate their conduct based solely on the *possibility* that they were being watched.

It's easy to argue that social media is our modern-day Panopticon. It is impossible to know who is watching you, and we filter our online behaviors based on the off chance that someone might be looking. It forces us to see ourselves the way the watchers do. We are both the guards and the prisoners, judging others while allowing others to judge us.

On these nights in the box, when the glass operates like a mirror, the only thing I can see is myself. I get to observe myself, judge myself, see myself as they do—as this woman does—from the outside, looking in.

It's hard not to wonder on those nights, seeing myself sitting there, stuck in a box, is this valid? Putting young women in glass boxes? Have I surrendered myself as an object for others to ogle? Am I someone who willingly objectifies herself?

Marina Abramović, the performance artist, has always used her body as the subject, medium, and object of her art. For her piece entitled "The Artist Is Present," Abramović sat in silence for more than seven hundred hours while strangers stared at her. For seven hours a day, from mid-March until the end of May, she sat motionless in an armless wooden chair, inside the atrium at The Museum of Modern Art in Manhattan. Anyone who wanted to (and was willing to wait in the sometimes overnight line) could sit opposite her, for as long as they liked, if they agreed to sit silently and motionless, too, and stare back into her eyes.

People often ask of Abramović's work, is it art? And perched like a doll in a display case, I have to wonder the same: Is this? Am I, too, performing in here? I'd like to think so. I'd like to think I'm playing an important part in an ongoing installation. But am I just deluding myself? Because if that's the case, then why the scanty outfits? Let's be honest, here. Am I a piece of art or a piece of ass?

However artistic an endeavor I may have assured myself this is, the strangers in the lobby don't necessarily see it that way. They see a girl on exhibit, clad in very little clothing, and they must think this is just another typically LA gimmick. Am I no different than the strippers down the street at The Body Shop?

I've asked a lot of people about this. While some feel the box is just a cheap, Hollywood attempt at grabbing attention, others, fortunately, see it as something more substantial. A friend told me one day, "What's so intriguing about the girls in the box is that they are *not* dancing, or posing seductively. For the most part, they are reading." This, she said, "Makes them that much more attractive."

During our first trip to LA, that summer after college, Rachel, Heather, and I went to The Standard. We had dinner in its twenty-four-hour diner with some guys we knew from college, and as we were leaving, we noticed the box. I said what I thought the people I was with wanted to hear, something like, "Oh my god, can you believe that? Weird. I mean, can you imagine?" But as the sliding-glass doors clicked open, I couldn't help but look back one more time, thinking, *That is so awesome.*

It's as if being a Box Girl is some strange LA badge of honor. And in that weird way, I like being seen in the box. I like this recognition. Attention is seductive, intoxicating. That is a hard thing to admit. That's not something you're supposed to admit.

But writers, after all, are performers. Though we are more bashful about it than actors who stand on stage and shout their talent to the world, the art and craft of writing is still a performance. Yet I spend the majority of my days sitting in front of a computer, by myself, staring out a window. It is an incredibly isolating way to make a living. (Or, almost make a living.) When I write in the box, in a sense, there is an audience. It is my stage.

The box also feeds my impulse to watch, and to record. I can observe—stealthily—but I don't have to engage. I am surrounded by the action and armed with a pen, but I'm not forced to join in. I get to report from inside this world. Like Joan Didion and Tom Wolfe and Lillian Ross and Gay Talese and all the other reporters I have admired all my life, I get to be a true fly on the wall. But unlike all of them, no one is questioning my tape recorder. Because of this, I like to think that I am using the box as much as it is using me. I like to think it's my little experiment. I get to know what it's like to be a creature in captivity that is pointed at and talked about by passing tourists. I get to be the monkey at the zoo—the monkey at the zoo with a human-sized brain and a laptop. They might be watching me, but I am watching them, too.

Women often ask if I feel vulnerable with all those people looking at me. The truth is, I feel powerful. Proud, even. This, I think, has everything to do with overcoming certain eating and body issues. So, in some ways, I have this sense of pride that I am finally at a point in my life where I can sit in a box in very little clothing and look good, knowing it's not because I deprived myself or ran twelve miles, but because I am actually, finally, healthy. I can wear this scanty outfit with triumph.

It has to be noted, though, that while The Standard has locations in Miami and New York, its Hollywood location is the only one with a box. Which is no surprise, really, given LA is a city that often seems entirely focused on external beauty, eternal youth, and so on. I'll pull the F. Scott Fitzgerald quote from my dad's photocopied page of *Forbes*: "Only remember—west of the Mississippi: it's a little more look, see, act. A little less rationalize, comment, talk." I used to believe this when I first moved to LA. I loved this quote. I took pride in it. I'd think, *I'm from the part of the country where people's brains are more valued than their bodies.* It took no time, however, to realize that there were as many artistic, intelligent, and interesting people on the "left coast" as on the right. And look at me now: a writer moonlighting as a Box Girl, relying on body, not brains. I'm sure tourists at the hotel assume I'm some bimbo, and you know what? I deserve that, for initially and irresponsibly writing off Los Angeles, its people, and its intellect. It's a city of countless contradictions, and perhaps for that reason above all others, it's a city that speaks to me so strongly.

Even from a geographical perspective, Los Angeles is a city mired in contradiction, the urban planning itself a dismembered mess of patchwork: Silverlake, Sherman Oaks, Westwood, Watts . . . Hollywood, Hawthorne, Brentwood, Bel Air . . . Koreatown, Compton, Marina del Rey. These neighborhoods have as much to do with one another as they do with Des Moines. Downtown Los Angeles is not even really downtown. Or maybe it is? It's impossible to tell. With its labyrinthine webs of expressways, LA is a city that is impossible to figure out. For my first year here, I didn't even know there was anything east of Fairfax Avenue. I had gone to the Farmer's Market, and to The Grove, and I thought that was it. I didn't know there was anything else over there. Unlike in Oakland, where Gertrude Stein says, "There's no there, there," in LA, there are countless theres, there. It just takes a while to find them.

Because of the city's fragmentary, far-flung floor plan, accessible almost exclusively by car, there is no collective sense of community, no overarching sense of "we." Unlike in New York, or Boston, or Chicago, where there is civic pride in spades, in LA, there is no central rallying cry. It's a city of transplants. When I meet someone who is actually from LA, my reaction is, "Really? You're whole life?" I want to put my friend Madison in a museum. (But that's also because her dad arrested O.J.) Everyone moves to LA with plans not to stay. But then we stay. Because somewhere along the way, this Garden of Forking Freeways burrows itself inside our hardened, from-elsewhere hearts, and slowly, we begin to love the place we claimed to hate.

Los Angeles is such a misunderstood city. I certainly didn't understand it at first—made assumptions about it, wrote it off. It's a place that's impossible not to ridicule until you really grit your teeth and muscle through the first two years. Truly, I think it takes that long to fully comprehend what's so redeeming about the place, and to fully appreciate all its endearing inconsistencies. It is ugly, and it is also beautiful. It is fast; it is slow. It is sexy, and it is also smart.

■

I grew up in a house full of contradictions. My mom pulls for University of North Carolina, my dad likes N.C. State. My mom is a bleeding heart liberal; my dad thinks Sarah Palin is a "babe." My dad believes in getting to the airport two hours before flight time; my mom once missed a flight while getting a manicure in the terminal. My mom would go to a cocktail party every night of the week; my dad likes to joke that he wants to move to a lighthouse. Every election year, they almost get divorced. My dad will walk into the kitchen and say, "I'm not staying in this room if Al Sharpton is on the TV. I have absolutely no patience for Al Sharpton." And my mom will laugh while turning up the volume. My parents also almost get divorced at the end of every college basketball season. During March Madness, my mom watches the games hunched over the kitchen counter—always in her lucky Carolina blue sweater—her eyes six inches away from the twelve-inch screen, screaming obscenities. While a perfect Southern lady eleven months of the year, come March, my mom starts talking like a character from *Road House*. A die-hard UNC fan, during tournament time, those "shit bags from Duke" are always up to no good. While my dad spends his Sundays watching every single golf tournament that is ever televised ("He would watch the Toilet Bowl Open, if it were on," my mom likes to say), his passion for college basketball these days is pretty lackluster. I once called the house and asked what they were up to, and my mom said, "Well, I'm in the kitchen watching college basketball, and your father's in the den watching *The Sound of Music*."

In all my years with the two of them, I have yet to uncover anything they have in common or any particularly compelling reason they ever got together. And still, they have been happily married for more than thirty years. That's not to say they don't have their fair share of arguments. But in some ways, I think the occasional knock-down, drag-out dispute is a sign of a good relationship. At least you're talking to each other. They say silence kills more relationships than violence. I don't remember who this "they" was, and while I'm pretty sure shooting someone with a shotgun or running them over with your car is a surefire way to end things, the sentiment still holds some merit. I don't trust couples who say they don't argue. It's like girls who don't drink beer; something's up. Somehow, after decades of being married to my dad, my mom hasn't poisoned the Metamucil, and I truly think it has something to do with their differences. They have amicably agreed to disagree.

I grew up a kind of contradiction myself. I was Southern. I was Northern. My Georgia friends teased me that I was a Yankee and my Connecticut friends called me a hick. To this day, if I say I am from Georgia in front of Connecticut friends, I get in trouble. If I say I grew up in Connecticut in front of my Southern friends, they want to give me a good ole fashioned ass whoopin'. But I don't care. I embrace it. I have always liked being the person from the other place.

Because of this, I have always been drawn to contradictions. I like the girl who works at a strip club and is also a Rhodes Scholar. I don't know if this girl exists, but if she does, I'd like to meet her. That girl has stories. To me, that girl is more honest, more real, than the girl who painstakingly crafts every aspect of her life to fit some perceived intellectual or artistic ideal. Where every book in her apartment, every artfully shot picture on Instagram, feeds some manufactured image. To me, that is more self-aware, more superficial, and way too self-serious. Do what makes you happy. Don't like what you think other people like. Because who cares, really? My friends have always been a rainbow coalition of characters from all walks of life (count it: two clichés, one sentence), because I've basically only ever had one requirement: You have to have a sense of humor about it all. You can't take yourself too seriously.

■

One afternoon I was having coffee with a writer friend in Echo Park and she asked, "What does your boyfriend do?" I said, "He works in finance. Or real estate. Or both. I'm not really sure how to describe it. He has a real job."

She said, "Oh," stabbing a straw into her iced coffee.

This was not an "Oh" like, "Oh! How cool." It was an "Oh" like, "Oh, gross."

The book *Hopscotch* by Argentine writer Julio Cortázar was written in Paris and published in Spanish. It is a book that has multiple endings, multiple interpretations, and can be read both front to back and back to front. I am not going to pretend this book was easy to follow, or particularly fun to read, but there was one paragraph that spoke to me, so I scribbled it down on one of the countless and uncontainable pieces of paper that follow me through my life:

> *As if the species in every individual were on guard against letting him go too far along the road of tolerance, intelligent doubt, sentimental vacillation. At some given point the callus, the sclerosis, the definition is born: black or white, radical or conservative, homo- or heterosexual, the San Lorenzo team or the Boca Juniors, meat or vegetables, business or poetry.*

Maybe, in the box, I function as a piece of art. Maybe, in the box, I'm just a piece of ass. Maybe I am neither. Maybe I am both. Maybe we don't have to decide. Maybe it doesn't matter. Maybe it's too hard to analyze something when you're sitting inside it.

Maybe, as my dad likes to say, the most honest answer someone can give is, "I don't know."

Maybe, I don't know.

Mom-Like

■

The assistant at the commercial agency called to tell me I had a last-minute audition for a Budweiser commercial later that afternoon. He recited the usual rundown: time, address, what to wear. At first I thought he said the wardrobe was a "skin-tight dress," but I was relieved when he repeated that it was a "mom-like dress." And then I was sort of disturbed. Had I really entered into the "mom" category of the casting world? I wasn't even thirty. And since when are there mom-types in beer commercials anyway?

I headed to my closet, dressed in fluorescent orange shorts and a cropped Red Hot Chili Peppers T-shirt. *I don't even like the Red Hot Chili Peppers*, I thought, scratching my unwashed hair. *Where did I acquire this shirt? And why is it cropped? This is not a "mom-like" thought*, I thought. *Moms know where their clothes come from. Right?*

I swatted through my closet, which was so overstuffed, my clothes actually wrinkled on the hangers. To my surprise, I realized I had a lot of "mom-like" dresses. (Most of them had been my mom's.) But what sort of "mom" were we talking about? A tan and toned, Lululemon-clad So-Cal mom? A Talbot's-sporting PTA-board-member East Coast mom? Or any number of mom-types in between? Being a mom for the first time was very confusing. I opted for a conservative yet form-flattering wrap dress. My mom (of the Talbot's school) has told me many times, "Nothing flatters a figure better than a good wrap dress, especially with a three-quarter-length sleeve!"

After slapping on my wrap dress, I combed some baby powder through my hair because I didn't have time to wash it. I must have squeezed the bottle a bit too eagerly, though, as a giant powdery cloud enveloped my head, turning my blonde to a lovely shade of frosted gray. I looked in the mirror. All of a sudden, I'd gone from "fresh young mom" to "hot grandmother who's had lots of plastic surgery." I flipped my head upside-down, attempting to shake the elderly out of my hair.

■

I am currently at that cruel crossroad in a woman's life when you start to get wrinkles but you haven't stopped getting the occasional zit. I recently went to an upscale skincare store and loaded up on proper products. I had always just used the stuff from the drugstore, but nearing thirty, I decided I needed to step up my skincare game. I also decided I should get the occasional facial.

About half way through one of these facials, the aesthetician told me I needed to "stop doing that with my face," or it was going to stay that way.

"Stay what way?" I popped up to my elbows, two saturated cotton pads falling off my eyes and landing in my lap.

She held up a hand mirror and pointed at the fleshy troughs between my eyebrows. *Oh my god*, I thought, *I look like a Pound Puppy.*

"I didn't even know I was doing that."

"You've been doing it the whole time."

This is probably because I don't find facials very fun, all that picking and poking and extracting. I raised my eyebrows as high as they would go to smooth the Pound Puppy ripples, and this left my forehead looking like a layer cake.

She coached me through some exercises to relax my face.

"La la la" she said, while flicking her tongue in and out of her mouth like a salamander.

"La la la," I said, while flicking my tongue in and out of my mouth like a salamander. "Do you know the sound a horse makes?" she asked.

"Neigh?" I answered.

"No, the other noise."

"Wait, I do know this one!"

I pressed my lips together and made a noise like a motor-boat. The aesthetician and I made the horse/motor boating noise at each other for a few minutes, split flying everywhere.

Since that facial, when I catch myself making the face that might make my face get stuck that way, I'll start doing the horse noise and flicking my tongue in and out of my mouth like a salamander. Normally I do this in the privacy of my own home, though I'm also not afraid to do it in the false-sense-of-privacy of my own car. People passing me on the road probably think I have Tourette's.

■

Flipping my head right side up, I glanced once more at my reflection and smacked some youthful, melon-colored lip gloss on my mouth. With that, I grabbed my purse—also my mom's—and headed to my audition.

Weltschmerz

Thumb-tacked to the bulletin board beside my desk is a small, square piece of paper that reads, "weltschmerz," written in my handwriting with ballpoint pen. The piece was pulled from the tower-like notepad my mom keeps next to the phone in the kitchen, for jotting down messages. One night, many years ago, I was sitting in that kitchen watching The National Spelling Bee. It was early evening in late summer, one of those days that feels like it's never going to end; something that thrilled me as a child. But during that long, confusing summer, dark couldn't come fast enough. It was the August after I graduated from college, and I was in the throes of a self-diagnosed "quarter-life crisis." I stared at the TV that night in the same catatonic state I had stared at my computer screen all summer. I'd sit at my desk, a plate of food on my lap, and incessantly hit the refresh button of my inbox, waiting for responses from jobs I'd applied to. Occasionally, convinced my email wasn't working, I'd send a message to one of my friends who already had a job.

Yep, I got your email, they'd reply. *Hey listen can I get back to you later? I'm really busy.*

"Sure," I'd say out loud. "Sure you can." Then I'd contemplate my options for the rest of the day: help my dad organize the recyclables in the garage before his weekly trip to the dump, or accompany my mom to Curves. I could have asked to borrow the car, I suppose. But where would I have gone? All my friends either already had jobs in New York or were also half-dead, staring at their computer screens, eating their parents' food. These were petty problems, I know. I was living at home with parents who were more than able and willing to take care of me. But that just made me feel more pathetic.

One morning, while watching a commercial for *The New York Times,* I let out a long, dramatic sigh and said to no one in particular, "I wish I had time to read *The New York Times* every day." My dad looked up from his *Wall Street Journal* and responded, "You do." But somehow I couldn't seem to find the time. The needing to get a job, the needing to figure out "what I was going to do with the rest of my life" was overwhelming. Because there was so much to figure out, I just let the paralysis consume me. Late at night, I'd crawl out my bedroom window onto the roof and look at the stars because it seemed like something to do. I was brooding. I was depressed. Or I wanted to be. Then, at least, I would have had an excuse to be loafing around in such a ridiculous condition. I was so pitiful, one night I burst into tears while watching a Staples back-to-school commercial. I missed my friends. I missed school. I did not like this new phase one bit.

I understand, of course, how insipid this all sounds. But that is the problem with being a member of the most self-absorbed, entitled generation in decades. We were reared on '90s catchphrases like "The sky's the limit!" and "You go girl!" As a woman—as an anyone, actually—I was lucky to be at this crossroads with so many choices. But I was overwhelmed by all of the roads. Never had my life been so in my control, yet never had I felt so out of control. It was like a *Choose Your Own Adventure* book, but instead of "If you want to slay the dragon, jump to page 47," it was, "If you want to go to law school, if you want to join the Peace Corps, if you'd like to be a lift operator in Vail . . ." I mean, I could have even been president. The year was 2004. Look at Hillary, look at Condi, *you go girl!* And of course, it's a great thing that we've come so far. When my mom's generation graduated from college (if they went at all), their choices were much more limited. Most of my mom's friends moved from college back to their home-towns in Georgia to marry their high school sweethearts and have babies. My mom did not. She's always been an extremely independent woman, a free thinker, and a hell of a champion for liberal causes, even among her almost entirely Republican friends (and husband). When she graduated from college (in three years), she moved out of Georgia and enrolled in grad-uate school at The University of North Carolina in Chapel Hill, where she got a master's degree in biology. Afterward, in Georgia, she got a job teaching high school science (and Sex Ed, for which she almost got fired), and bought an apartment. All on her own. My dad did it all on his own, too. He paid his way through college with academic scholarships (and sometimes by donating blood) and put himself through business school. When his job transferred him from Georgia to New Jersey in the late '80s, he uprooted all of us—me, six; my brother, nine—to a place we'd never heard of: Connecticut. I knew it only as one of the small pieces on my United States puzzle that was always missing. But he went where the opportunity was. My parents think you do the most with what you have. You go as far as you can go. Yet at twenty-two, this sentiment just made me all the more anxious and confused. It was like the toothpaste aisle at the grocery store. I don't want seventeen choices. I want toothpaste. While I desperately wanted to be an adult, I still felt like a kid. I just wanted someone to tell me what to do, to just give me my goddamn toothpaste.

■

Watching TV in the kitchen that night, I listened as the National Spelling Bee contestant—no older than twelve and, as far as I was concerned, much more accomplished than me—asked for the definition of "weltschmerz." When the moderator recited it, I leapt from my chair to get a pen, so taken by its meaning: "sentimental depression about the actual state of the world versus an ideal state." It was a German word, of course. They always have the best words to describe the worst things. I wrote down the word and its definition. I was delighted. Now I had a sophisticated, final-round-of-The-National-Spelling-Bee word, from the Germanic, to describe what was wrong with me.

I'm omitting some important details. I'd like to leave them out—I was trying to leave them out—but I can't. It just creates too many holes. This post-matriculation meltdown was caused by more than just being bummed that my friends were now scattered across the country and my journalism degree from a top-five party school was never going to get me a job. I was also in love with a guy who lived three thousand miles away and was not my boyfriend. He was one of those friends from college that I was so heartbroken to let go of. And was I that in love with him in retrospect? I don't really know. What I do know is that I was not ready to move to Manhattan to marry my boyfriend, who was twenty-eight (or "thirty minus two," as my girlfriends sometimes called him). I had just turned twenty-two, and I was terrified. All of the movie clichés I'd ever heard—*that I felt like I could see my whole life laid out before me*—seemed like they were written just for me. When Rose whimpered from the bow of the *Titanic*, "I saw my whole life as if I'd already lived it," I thought, *You go girl*. I, too, could see it all: the engagement party in the city, the fourteen-bridesmaid wedding, the house in Greenwich, the kids, the carpool route, the yellow lab named "Bear" or "Buck." And while both of these guys were good people, this really had nothing to do with either of them. It was—cue yet another relationship cliché—about me. I just wasn't ready for the relationship that fast-tracked me into adulthood.

So I ran away. I broke up with the New York boyfriend, blindsiding him and everybody else by moving to California. Looking back, this move wasn't so much for the other guy (though he did conveniently live there, and we did end up dating for a little bit). It was an escape from a life I wasn't ready to live. My parents were heartbroken, and I was, too—that I had made them that way. But I knew I had to go. I was as close to having a nervous breakdown as I ever wanted to come, and I'd already promised my girlfriends anyway. We were all suffering from various degrees of the quarter-life crisis, and we were certain a dramatic change of scenery was the only solution. In our less melancholy moments, my parents and I were able to make light of it: I was suffering from a quarter-life crisis with a side of bi-coastal disorder. Much like the quarter-life crisis, bi-coastal disorder included symptoms such as sobbing while repeatedly listening to Kelly Clarkson's "Breakaway" and the theme song to *The O.C.* So, my girlfriends and I packed up our clothes and books and beds, boarded them on a Penske truck, and promised our parents we'd only be there a year, no more than two.

But that's not what happened. It never is. And now I understand, as Joan Didion learned, how six months could become eight years. Tacked to the same wall as "weltschmerz" is a line from Didion's essay "Goodbye To All That," written in red pen on a torn-off corner of a yellow legal pad page: "That was the year, my twenty-eight, when I was discovering that not all of the promises would be kept, that some things are in fact irrevocable and that it had counted after all, every evasion and every procrastination, every mistake, every word, all of it." I was exactly twenty-eight when I read that for the first time, and I immediately broke down into tears. How had I not read it sooner? Why had no one told me to? During my first year in California, I sporadically kept a journal, and on one of its pages I wrote: "I wish someone would just tell me where I'd be in ten years so I could stop worrying about it."

More than that, I wish someone had told me at twenty-two, twenty-three—even twenty-five—what Didion finally figured out. That all of it—even the mistakes and the procrastinations—would count. I wish someone had told me that it would all work out, eventually. That it might take a hell of a lot longer than I thought it would, and that it certainly wouldn't go the way I expected it to. That I would have more jobs and more apartments than I could count on two hands. (In eight years, I moved seven times.) That I would have much, much joy and many disappointments, many highs, and as many hangovers. That I would get over the ones that I thought were The Ones. That, at certain points, jobs would let me down, relationships would let me down, the government would let me down, friends would let me down. That I would think it was cool to be broke until I would no longer think it was cool to be broke. That several things I believed with all of my being—believed so vehemently that I would pound my fist on a barroom table until my micro-brewed beer spilled out of its glass—I would completely disagree with only a few years later. That my twenties would last for fifty years. That a lot can change in fifty years.

■

I don't know when it was decided that thirty was the year. Maybe over a caboodle of Barbies on Kimberly Baker's living room rug. After cramming Ken in the driver's seat of the pink Corvette (in which the bulky, albeit penis-less Ken never seemed to fit) and placing his golf clubs in the backseat, we'd wave Barbie's rubbery arm from beneath the pink, plastic portico of their mansion. Being a good wife, Barbie would always wave until Ken was down the road and out of sight. Meaning, behind the couch. Then we'd scurry her through the front door; she had to change out of her apron and into something sportier because Skipper was coming over to help her pick out her outfit for the ball that night. (Basically all our Barbies ever did was say goodbye to their husbands and try on outfits for whatever nighttime activity was planned for their return.) In our minds, Barbie had it all: the mansion, the convertible, the closet (though now I realize she actually didn't have a closet, just a pile of clothes that was half the height of the house), the endless social engagements, and a best pal named Skipper who never seemed to have plans of her own but was always more than willing to help Barbie primp for hers. We'd sit there sipping Citrus Cooler Capri Suns, our Gumby-like knees bent out to the side in a position that would be entirely impossible to get into (or out of) now, and plan our lives.

"When we're thirty," we'd say, because it was always thirty, "we'll move in next door to each other, and our kids will play in the cul-de-sac, and our husbands will play golf, and we'll try on clothes." It was the all-American dream, pre-packaged for us by Mattel.

Years later, in adolescence, it was still thirty. "If we don't find anyone else to marry by the time we're thirty," I'd say, to my best guy friend, "Then we'll marry each other."

And even at twenty, it was still thirty. One night while dancing on the bar at a saloon in South Georgia, I reached for Melissa's wrist to hoist her up. "Come on!" I shouted over Def

Leppard's "Pour Some Sugar On Me," my swollen, beer-fat body stuffed into a sundress, my shoulders magenta because this was also before I wore sunscreen. "We can't do stuff like this when we're thirty!" Since that night, I have been made fun of for this line way more than thirty times.

■

One night, not long ago, the foursome from that first house in Santa Monica reunited for dinner in LA. It was a rare treat to have us all in the same city—by that point, we were strewn all over the country. Heather had moved to New York for an even better producer position, Melissa was in New York for law school, Rachel was enjoying a successful career designing children's clothing San Francisco (yay, painting degree!), and I was still in LA. During dinner, we talked about my impending "big" birthday. It seemed like I was supposed to be upset about it—thirty, the big 3-0, the end of the line, the party's over—but all I could think was, *Thank god.* If anything, I was relieved to be getting out of my twenties. How many lives had I lived during this interminable decade anyway? Five? Fifteen?

Like me, they weren't particularly upset about thirty either. We'd always prided ourselves on being "fiercely independent" women, and quite frankly, we were tired of being "fierce" and "independent." While at one point the thought of living anywhere but New York, LA, or San Francisco sounded simply pedestrian, we found ourselves at thirty talking romantically about cities somewhere in between. Longing for lives more pastoral, slower paced. The phrase "a farm in Wisconsin" was said, as well as "the burbs of Chicago." Even "Kansas City," for chrissake. After nine lives worth of tiny apartments, failed relationships, too little money, and too little sleep, these places started sounding idyllic, a suburban Valhalla. *Just give me a good coffee maker, a laptop, a Tahoe, and a carpool route,* I thought. And as soon as I thought that, I was haunted by one of my many former selves: Isn't that exactly what I was running away from when I moved to California? But that was then. And if it weren't for all that living in between, I would have resented it, rejected it. Freaked out.

What was it then? Were we feeling maternal? For being so independent—*make them chase us, don't call back, don't text first*—at thirty, did we really just want a husband, a house, and a couple of kids? In an attempt to be less of a mess, I now occasionally record snapshots from my day in Word documents and save them in a folder on my desktop titled "Notes." The documents have titles like: "Notes on Technology," "Notes on LA," "Notes on Dad."

One of them is "Notes On Nightmares About Babies":

Losing my babies under beach towels at the pool.
My nephew's head keeps falling off when I hold him.
Does this mean I'm not ready to have children?
Is this normal?

Needless to say, this desire for a downshift was not necessarily maternal. It is interesting though, that when my mom was twenty-nine, she already had one child and one was on the way, yet she still felt way behind the curve. That was the early '80s in Augusta, Georgia, though. My mom didn't marry until she was twenty-four and, at that age, was considered an old maid. This must have had something to do with the fact that every Christmas after college, she had to be "re-presented" to society at something called The Spinsters Ball.

"The *Spinsters* Ball?" I repeated, on the phone. "The name alone."

The Spinsters Ball was a black-tie gala at the country club, my mom explained, with the sole purpose of announcing to the whole town which women were still single. "About halfway through the night," she said, "they got the crowd's attention, and everyone gathered around the ballroom floor. The master of ceremonies called out our names, and we all stood in a sort of semicircle, and everyone applauded."

My mouth was agape.

"So that was sort of embarrassing," she added. She told me they sent an engraved invitation every year, inviting her to participate.

"Well could you turn it down?" I asked.

"Oh no you didn't turn it down," she said. "It was considered an honor to be invited."

The Spinsters Club was the sister society to The Bachelors Club, but, as my mom told me, "All *they* did was throw one heck of a costume ball. They were just out to have a good time." As bachelors typically are. (Again, the name alone.) My mom was twenty-three when she made her final appearance at The Spinsters Ball. "I said, 'If I am not engaged by this time next year, I am *not* doing this again.'" Fortunately, my dad proposed that spring. I sort of wish he hadn't, though. I would have loved to know if she would have kept that promise.

Because a twenty-three-year old never keeps the promises she makes. She's never the same person she was a year before. As I approach thirty, I feel lighter, shedding all those selves. I survived my twenties—the ecstatic highs and pathetic lows, the forty-pound weight gain while studying abroad, the over-tweezed eyebrows and the tanning-bed tans, George W. Bush (and the insisting we'd move to France if he was reelected, but, of course, the never moving). I survived the mistakes, the regrets, the firsts, the lasts, the baby tees and flare-leg jeans. I made it through the hippie phase, the preppy phase, the hipster phase, and even the asymmetrical mullet.

■

At dinner that night, we sat around an outdoor table drinking wine, laughing about some of the dumber things our younger selves did during the last decade. We talked about how the only time Melissa had ever gone commando in her life was also the time her wraparound skirt busted open at the top of a staircase during a party. We talked about the time Rachel nearly burned down her apartment after preheating the oven to make a midnight snack, then fell asleep and forgot she was also using her oven as a storage space for a Costco-sized barrel of pretzels. We talked about the time Heather's car was stolen while she was throwing up red wine in the bathroom at Chez Jay in Santa Monica. And then, of course about the time I lit my face on fire, along with a large section of a tablecloth, at the Nobu in Las Vegas—while attempting to take their signature flaming sambuca shot, the hairs on my upper lip charred into a John Waters mustache.

And who knows? I thought as the night continued. *Maybe ten years from now, we'll be circled around another table littered with wine glasses, longing for our twenties. Those wild and unbridled days before daycare and diapers, mortgages and divorces.*

Our service at the restaurant that night was terrible. Our server might as well have just gone out the back door and never come back because we would have gotten more attention that way. Someone else would have come over and asked if we'd like something else, which we did—much, much more wine. But, because they thought we were in good hands, no one ever came over. We sat at the table surrounded by empty wine glasses, and because we are women who hadn't seen each other in a long time, we kept talking and talking, but—let's be honest—we would have much preferred if our glasses were full, not empty. What can I say? We're optimists.

After an hour of no one asking if we'd like more wine, more water, a dessert, anything, our server reemerged and causally tossed off a, "Can I get you anything else?" I placed my hands on the table, flipped them palms up, and motioned toward the four empty wine glasses stained the color of old, dried blood. Then I replied, in my most scolding tone, "Well, we would have liked something else but at this point"—I raised my hands even higher to indicate *I give up*—"You should probably just bring us the check." Our server's eyes popped out of her head like a scared little frog that was about to get stepped on, and said she'd be right back with our check. She scurried out of sight to get our bill and to no doubt talk about what a bitch that girl on table ten had been.

Oh god, I thought, *oh god oh god oh god, did I really just act like that? Have I become one of those women who I used to hate waiting on?* I looked around the table. We were all drinking wine; two of us had also ordered cups of herbal tea. One of us was wearing a leopard print top. (Sure, animal print was sort of "in," but still.) We had spent the majority of the night talking about men and aging. We were definitely those women.

When our server returned with our check, I thought to myself, *I know this girl. She is young, in her early twenties, just embarking on this exhausting adventure. She's not a good waitress, no, but good for her. She has other ambitions. She has a whole decade of mistakes and false starts, several lifetimes to figure it all out.*

We threw four credit cards on the table, then discussed how many dollars below twenty percent we should leave her:

"I don't think she deserves more than ten percent."

"We could have walked up the street to Whole Foods and gotten wine faster."

"We could have stomped and fermented our own wine faster."

"I think I'm going to become a member of Yelp just so I can complain about her service."

While exchanging goodbyes by the front door, I said I left

my phone on the table. Making sure no one saw me, I pulled a twenty from my wallet and left it on top of the credit card slips.

■

When I look at old pictures of us from our early twenties, with the ashy matte makeup and the bad, blunt haircuts, I don't think we look good. Yet when I look at the pictures from that night, I think, *We're glowing.* Maybe this is because we finally discovered good moisturizers and learned to consume more water than just the club soda in our vodka drinks. But more than that, in those old photos, we just look tired. It's the same thing when I look at old pictures of me sitting in the box. I don't think, wow, I look young. I think, wow, I look exhausted. I was living so many lives then. Standing at the threshold to thirty, I was looking forward to only living one.

■

Soon after that dinner, a group of men struck up a conversation with some friends and me at a restaurant bar in Palm Desert. The men were older, gray-haired, married. One worked in LA and knew the box at The Standard well. When he found out I was occasionally a Box Girl, he said, "Aren't you a little too old to be in the box?"

This would have sent me into a tailspin a few years before. *Oh god. Do I look old? Am I getting old?* The younger me would have shot back something surly about his gray hair and how he should talk. But my near-thirty self just raised my glass, laughed, and said, "Probably."

And maybe I finally am.

The Concierge Desk

Two men are working at the front desk tonight. Their backs are toward me. They're wearing white button-down shirts with subtle silver pinstripes, white pants, and white, rubber-soled shoes, which look geriatric. On the desk are two computers, two phones, two credit card machines, two printers, a cup holding pens, and an industrial-sized container of wet wipes. I can see everything on the concierges' computer screens. They must realize this. Maybe not? They used to spend hours looking at MySpace. Now, Facebook. I sometimes wonder what they did before MySpace. Did they talk to each other?

Right now, the one directly in front of me isn't even standing up straight. He's hunched over, his left elbow next to the keyboard, his right hand on the mouse, just scrolling down pages, clicking through Facebook pictures. Over and over again. When the phone rings he answers, "Hello, Standard!" still scrolling and trolling.

To the left of the front desk is the deejay booth. Tonight the deejay is a tiny, Tinkerbell-like girl with close-cropped pixie hair. She is adorable. She looks like she could live inside someone's pocket. She dances a dainty little dance while she deejays, subtly shifting her shoulders from side to side while her right hand rests on the turntable. But it's not a turntable. There are no records. There are two record-like circles with a Macbook in between. On the laptop's screen, neon green lines pulse up and down like the machine at the hospital that beeps and blips and tells you whether someone's dead or alive.

It is late and no one has come into the lobby for a while. Toward the end of the night, other staff members gather around the front desk. The valet guy comes in and asks the concierge how Vegas was. The tiny deejay takes off her headphones and turns toward the front desk to chat. I am not a part of this conversation. I am behind this conversation. I am as much a part of the background as the ambient music the deejay is playing. They are ignoring me as much as I am ignoring them. Except I'm not ignoring them.

Deejay Girl excuses herself and tells the concierge to watch the turntables. He says he's going to put on Celine Dion. He seems to be a bit of a jokester. She twirls back toward him, giggles, and says, "You do that, I'll kill you," and slips into another part of the hotel.

Jokester Concierge starts singing Celine Dion's "My Heart Will Go On" while he wraps an iPhone cord around his hand. He is a very bad singer and he finds this very funny.

Deejay Girl returns with something that looks like a bowl of soup. It might not be soup. It's hard to tell if she's using a fork or a spoon.

Jokester Concierge, who is a bit hefty, announces he wants some dessert.

Deejay Girl turns back toward him and says, "My sister was just in town, with my niece who's two. She's at that age where she says anything that you tell her." She blows on the bowl. (It's soup.) "And she just says words really funny. Like when you tell her to say, 'vacuum,' it sounds like, 'fuck you.'" Jokester

Concierge erupts in laughter. I can't tell if he actually thinks it was that funny, or if he'd just like to make out with her.

I go back to reading until a boisterous group of guys stumble through the sliding glass doors and into the lobby. They seem very excited about the box. A flash bursts. Jokester Concierge shouts, "No pictures, no pictures, no pictures!" The one taking the pictures puts his phone in his back pocket. He is wearing a black button-down shirt with a dragon stitched on the shoulders. He says, "Sorry, man," and asks where the nearest liquor store is.

The group leaves for the liquor store and the lobby is empty again. Deejay Girl leans on the front desk with her chin propped on her right hand and says, "Okay, it's time to tell each other bad jokes." She starts. I can't hear the joke. Maybe it's dirty or racist, because she tells it very quietly. The concierge then tells some joke about a priest. The pocket-sized deejay laughs politely.

I go back to my magazine until I hear the word "heroin." Deejay Girl says she's from Baltimore originally, "But I had to get out of there, because everyone around me started doing heroin."

Jokester Concierge looks up from his computer and lets out a concerned-sounding, "*Dude.*" I don't think he runs in those circles.

"I've never used it," she says. "I've just seen people massively messed up on it. And that's why I decided to leave."

"Gnarly."

At eleven o'clock, Jokester Concierge is relieved by the grumpy older one who has been working here as long as I have. The fun stops. Deejay Girl returns to her tables and to looking at her iPhone.

I have never seen the grumpy concierge smile or speak unless directly addressed by a guest. He always seems very put out when I ask him to validate my valet ticket at the end of the night. He wears frameless glasses and is, at the moment, involved in a Google search for Bose noise-canceling headphones.

I've Got the Over on Fifteen Minutes

■

It's a bit bizarre to think that strangers have watched me sleep. Right now, a group of guys is placing bets on what time I will doze off. One of them points a Peroni at me.

"I've got the over on fifteen minutes," he says. "If she falls asleep before then, you're buying the next round."

Beer bottles clink. "Deal."

Tired

The lighting in the box is dim tonight, which is always nice (flattering for the thighs, good for sleeping). On the glass, the words, THE RAINBOW PROJECT are written in large, black-outlined letters, each one filled with a different color of the rainbow. There's a black-and-white barcode sketched after the letter T. Behind me, a rainbow is projected in a swirling pattern.

The dim, kaleidoscopic lighting is lulling me to sleep, like something in a child's nursery. Red, orange, yellow, green, blue, violet. Then black.

Almost black. A guy in a red long-sleeved University of Something T-shirt rolls a giant duffle bag up to the desk and starts barking at the concierge. Finally, he gets the answer that he's looking for and lugs his suitcase toward the elevator. A few minutes later, he's back, without the bag, sitting on a couch in the lobby. Straight in front of me. Just staring.

I really wish he wouldn't. Doesn't he know I'm trying to fall asleep?

Whitman

◾

It's late now, a quarter to two. Guys begin to trip out of the bar and toward the valet, with girls hanging on their arms in skirts so tight and short and heels so high, they don't walk so much as scoot. I eye one of the girls and think, *Her skirt is way too short. She looks like a whore.*

◾

Do I contradict myself? Then I contradict myself. I am large, I contain multitudes.

◾

Am I allowed to quote Whitman while sitting half-naked in the lobby of a hotel? Am I?

[ACKNOWLEDGMENTS]

I am profoundly grateful to Nicole Antonio, early box book champion and editor extraordinaire. If I said thank you once a day forever it still might not be enough. You are scary smart, seriously. I would like to also thank everyone else at Counterpoint/Soft Skull who devoted their time and talents to making this book what it is today: Liz Parker, Julia Kent, Kelly Winton, Megan Fishmann. And also: Barrett Briske, copy-editing wizard.

A sincere thanks to the faculty at the USC Master of Professional Writing program, and most especially Dinah Lenney, for her thoughtful readings and warm critique, and for wisely suggesting I chop this thing up, and make it a hybrid of sorts. Without that advice, I'm certain I'd still be slogging hopelessly through chapter two. A thanks is owed to Bernard Cooper, too, for forcing me to take myself, and this essay-turned-book, more seriously.

I'd like to thank the New York State Writers Institute at Skidmore, and Jim Miller in particular, for the early, hearty encouragement.

Of the non-professional variety: thanks to Melissa for reminding me to send my manuscript on Monday, to T.K. for the chair, and to C.K. for inspiring me daily.

Thank you to Peter, for giving me that course catalog for

my birthday so many years ago, putting a sticky note on the page for nonfiction classes, and writing: "Pick two." You make ordinary people do extraordinary things.

And finally, to my parents, and their parents, and the rest of my extended family: you are unintentionally some of the funniest people I know. And to my brother: you are intentionally one of the funniest people I know. Thank you all for boatloads of love and laughter.

[ABOUT THE AUTHOR]

Lilibet Snellings was born in Georgia and raised in Connecticut. She earned her MFA from the University of Southern California and currently lives in Chicago. Her work has appeared in *The Huffington Post*, *Los Angeles* Magazine, *Anthem*, *Flaunt*, and *This Recording*, among other publications.